HOMAGE

Poems and Prose
by
Charlotte Hill O'Neal aka Mama C
(Iya Osotunde Fasuyi)

African Perspectives Publishing
PO Box 95342, Grant Park 2051,
Johannesburg, South Africa
www.africanperspectives.co.za

© Charlotte Hill O'Neal
email: mamacharlottesmusic2@yahoo.com

ISBN PRINT: 978-1-77637-682-7
ISBN DIGITAL: 978-1-77637-683-4

Cover Image: Emma Maasai
Graphic Designer: Fuze Designs
Typesetting: Phumzile Mondlani

CONTENTS

DEDICATION

This collection of poems and prose is dedicated to my father, Mzee Sterling E. Hill, Sr. who recently passed away at the age of 94 years *'young'* as he would always remind us.

What a blessed spirit I am to be allowed to live in this paradise on earth, in the foothills of Mt Meru in a little village named Imbaseni!

As the morning clouds that shroud the top of that mountain start to open like curtains of folded memories, I can hear my dad's laughter and feel his humor as he calls out *'Pumpkin!'*

I know that all is well despite the tears ...

I pay HOMAGE to my Ancestors...

I pay HOMAGE to the Earth...
the Waters...
the Fire...
the Air...

and to the Spiritual Forces who guide and protect me...

Ase! Ase!

Ase O!

BOOK REVIEWS

'It's not everyday that we are blessed with a poetry compilation that encapsulates 13 years of work from an accomplished African activist elder. As the title suggests, *Homage* publicly gives honor and shows respect and admiration for a host of souls who have impacted the author Charlotte Hill O'Neal or Mama C as she is affectionately known by many.

In this collection of poems and writings, Hill O'Neal pays tribute to her parents, aunties, iconic historic figures such as Lil Bobby Hutton and others. She also gives insight into her world travels, such as her time spent in China, and writes about her life in Tanzania as a U.S. transplant. O'Neal sprinkles words from other languages throughout this book including Yoruba, KiSwahili and more which adds to the journey

In 2006, I had an opportunity to spend three weeks in Imbeseni Village with Mama C and her husband Pete O'Neal at the United African Alliance Community Center (UAACC) and witness the well that was installed largely thanks to Geronimo Ji Jaga Pratt as well as the solar work that was being done. I was able to sit in on classes taught by volunteers from around the world and work with resident artists. I took in Mama C's sculpture work, and participated in spoken word events and spontaneous jam sessions with Mama C's bandmates. Perhaps this influences how the work in *Homage* impacts me and is why my favorite piece in *Homage* is "Dreams of Kili and Beyond". While I had no desire to climb Mount Kilimanjaro, the mountain stands prominently and magnificently in view as you embark upon each day in the village. Other favorites in *Homage* include, "Don't let them take our joy/we are the knowers, the excerpt interview of Charlotte and Pete and the entire chapter of The China Experience".

While there is material here that may bring tears to your eyes, there are also entries that will uplift your spirit. Because the work is expansive, you are certain to encounter something here that will touch you at your core. Hill O'Neal even includes some erotica!

Congratulations on another great project completed Mama C! Imagine if we had a treasure such as this from all of our mothers and grandmothers. With this one, you are leaving a very important legacy for generations to come.'

Dr. V.S. Chochezi is a writer, poet, artist, photojournalist, certified Myers Briggs practitioner, and college professor. She is the daughter member of Straight Out Scribes, a renowned mother/daughter spoken word duo who have self-published seven books of poetry, one Sci-fi Anthology and two CD compilations. They have produced and coordinated a number of writing, poetry and art related programs and workshops in Sacramento since 1991. They have lent their voices to such causes as the Campaign to Save the Life of Mumia Abu-Jamal, freedom for the MOVE 9, Leonard Peltier, and other political prisoners. They have supported environmental causes, LGBTQIA+ rights, have performed for Black Family Day, Women Take Back the Night, Labor Unions, the Sacramento Thousand Man March, the Whole Earth Festival, numerous colleges and are members of ZICA Creative Arts and Literary Guild of Sacramento.

'As the world continues to struggle through a politicized pandemic featuring a cunning virus that generates a prolific daily death toll… as we, the historically disenfranchised, have initiated a global racial reckoning ignited by the televised lynching of our brother George Floyd… **Homage**, the latest collection of poetry and prose by Charlotte O'Neal (or "Mama C" as many of us call her) is the literary balm the world needs as we collectively seek a source of healing. Divided into six sections, the collection simultaneously takes the reader on a journey through Mama C's eyes and serves as a powerful memoir while also providing voyages to the Motherland, to China, and to the spiritual realm where one can re-connect with the Ancestors. In the opening sequence of poems, Homage to the Ancestors, Mama C introduces us to *Those Left Behind,* which serves as a tribute to the Ancestors whose loved ones were stolen during the Transatlantic slave trade:

> …it seems nobody talks about **those** Mothers
> who screamed and called out their daughter's names
> over and over each morning
> at the crack of dawn
> refusing to give into hopelessness
> even years after the terrible kidnappings

I am continually impressed by Mama C's ability to skillfully craft poetic lines that crackle with the urgency of decolonizing our minds. She makes it clear that honoring our ancestry is absolutely necessary to the struggle for liberation. In section two, *Homage to a Few Freedom Fighters*, I was delighted to find the poem, *Li'l Bobby… We Remember You,* which sings the praises of Li'l Bobby Hutton who, as Mama C notes, was the first official member of the Black Panther Party, gunned down and killed by police in Oakland, California at the age of 17. The poem celebrates the life of a brother the history books overlooked:

Still fresh images of Lil' Bobby...
stingy brimmed hat set at gravity defying angles
with just the right kind of tilt that let you know that this
brother was
Cooool!!
He was correct...
He was about some THING!

Subsequent sections include poems that give us insight into Mama C's incredible life, her lineage, a tribute to numerous matriarchs, and vivid accounts of her participation in a competitive writer's residency sponsored by the Shanghai Writers Association. She was the first African to be selected which gave her the opportunity to make her first trip to China in 2015. While Mama C wields the weapon of poetry to fight injustice, this stunning collection is also a profound source of encouragement. Listen to Mama C's admonishment in the poem *Don't Let Them Take Our Joy:*

Even in the midst of fighting back
we MUST experience Joy!
It is what charges our collective batteries!
NEVER let them take our joy away!
Even THAT is resistance!

Homage is an epic poetic journey that honors our ancestors and "charges our batteries" as we continue in the fight for true liberation.'

Glenn North is currently the Executive Director of the Bruce R. Watkins Cultural Heritage Center. He received an MFA in Creative Writing from UMKC. Glenn is the author of City of Song, a collection of poems inspired by Kansas City's rich jazz tradition and the triumphs and tragedies of the African American experience. He is a Cave Canem fellow, a Callaloo creative writing fellow and a recipient of the

Charlotte Street Generative Performing Artist Award and the Crystal Field Poetry Award.

North's work has appeared in the Langston Hughes Review, Kansas City Voices, One Shot Deal, The Sixth Surface, Caper Literary Journal, KC Studio, Cave Canem Anthology XII, The African American Review, and American Studies Journal. He collaborated with legendary jazz musician, Bobby Watson, on the critically acclaimed recording project, Check Cashing Day and is currently filling his appointment as the Poet Laureate of the 18th & Vine Historic Jazz District.

INTRODUCTION

I love to walk around the grounds of the United African Alliance Community Centre (UAACC). I love to look up at the towering trees (most of which we planted ourselves) and listen to the bush babies when they are going vocally berserk during their mating season. I actually thought for years that their eerily sing-song tunes were coming from BIRDS!! I couldn't figure out why birds were singing so strongly at night being that they were supposed to be asleep! And one day I finally saw three of the bush babies, who normally live raucous nocturnal lives, crying at the top of their voices, stranded in the afternoon sun and asking for help at the bottom of an elevated but uncovered and dry water tank. Actually, that reservoir had been our swimming pool for several years but during a drought one year we drained that chlorinated water and transformed it to serve as water storage. How could we even think to justify having a swimming pool in a village during a drought!

We ended up carefully putting a couple of long poles into the tank that day so that the little creatures could shyly climb out and return to the security of the tall trees.

We were elated that our efforts to assist those bush babies were successful!

SISI kwa SISI...WE ARE ONE!!

I know that community minded way of thinking continues to be informed by not only the life I lived as the child of hard working parents in Kansas City, but my experiences as a Black Panther Party Woman way back in the 60s and early 70s also has had a tremendous impact on the way I continue to live and breathe the spiritual essence of in Tanzania.

My husband, comrade and ultimate friend, Mzee Pete O'Neal's description of my very first poetry book titled WARRIOR WOMAN OF PEACE continues to ring true for this compilation, HOMAGE.

He *says "Charlotte combines spirituality, idealism and revolutionary fervor with painful Ancestral memories of the Middle Passage and the horrors of bondage. She weaves a haunting tapestry loaded with threads of self-pride and determination: She explores the depths of self-hate and dependency and she does not spare herself in this voyeuristic observation of the 'Inner-One' but instead uses her life experiences as proof that 'what was' does not have 'to be'. And throughout this book Charlotte generously flavors each piece with a compelling altruism and perhaps most importantly, the dynamic of love!"*

Mzee Pete got it RIGHT back in 2008...and he has hit the nail squarely on its head once more!

I bring you a gift to share from my Ancestors...I present HOMAGE!

I.   <u>HOMAGE TO ANCESTORS</u>

TEACH THE CHILDREN...

THE THING THAT WE SHOULD ALWAYS REMEMBER

THE THING THAT WE SHOULD NEVER EVER FORGET

IS THAT THE LOVE THAT WE WERE ALL

CONCEIVED OUT OF

HAS A HEALING POWER WHOSE LIGHT KEEPS US POWERFULLY

LIT...

REMEMBER...

AND

TEACH THE CHILDREN!

My Mother's Hands

Elegant
but marked with the corns on her fingers
that spoke of curling irons and straightening combs
from hours and hours and years and years
of *'doing hair'* in her beauty shop

Hands that were wrinkled and red and swollen sometimes
from being in dish water too long without the soothing balm of
Vaseline

Hands that coaxed the Creators voice to surround us
as she played the piano and made us hear the swish of angels' wings
when she got on her organ

Hands in the doorway of my room when she whispered,
"Why didn't you tell me Charlotte...why didn't you just tell me?"

Hands that held the switch
(that I had usually had to cut off the tree myself)
as she reluctantly, it seemed,
whipped some sense into my hard head

Hands that kept my hair neat and braided or curled
and made sure that my *kitchens* were always pressed out and shining

Hands that very seldom burnt me
even with all my ducking and dodging that hot comb sizzle

Hands that put sticky mustard plasters on my chest
and Vicks vapor rub up my nose
and rubbed my high temperatures down with alcohol

while she soothed my fevered brow
over and over with her gentle love touch

Hands that kept our clothes ironed and starched
and in brand new Easter duds every year
while SHE wore the same elegant red cape and suit
year in and year out

Hands that tearfully picked the *chit'lins* off the ceiling
after the pressure cooker exploded its contents one Sunday morning
and hung wriggling surrealistically off her newly painted white ceiling
that had the pretty gold flakes mixed in it

Hands that teased us with left over exotic food
like fried grasshoppers and chocolate covered ants
and phallic looking cows' tongues,
bought home from the rich white folks' parties she would waitress at
every summer with my aunts
to help make ends meet at home

Hands that whipped the batter over and over and over and over
to make sure that the cakes that she sold were as light as the luscious
dinner rolls she was so proud of
and that we were always so eager to devour

Hands that taught me to arch my eyebrows
and to fold my clothes
and which fork was which to use when

Hands that made the inexpensive dress she had found for me
to wear to the installation ceremony
feel like a million dollars
by simply pinning one of her brooches on it

Hands that lay limp and pale
but elegant still
as she took her last breath
and settled her face into a smile

My Mother's hands
elegant
knurled
smooth
cracked
rough
moist
strong
limp
soothing
creative
at rest

My Mother's Hands...Hands Full of Love!

Those Left Behind

...and nobody hardly EVER mentions the MOTHERS...
those whose sons and daughters were snatched away
and
chained and whipped and beat
into heavy, rusted
rough hewed metal
that tore flesh on tender perfumed necks
and
efun covered ankles and thighs...

...it seems nobody talks about **those** Mothers
who screamed and called out their daughter's names
over and over each morning
at the crack of dawn
refusing to give into hopelessness
even years after the terrible kidnappings

Who hears their hoarse and worn-out voices
drowning out the visions
of the flocks of crows and gatherings of bloated vultures
who repeatedly pecked out the soft eyeballs
and once tender sperm sacks
of the men who never made it to the bellies of those stinking, hellish
ships?

...and who thinks about those fathers
who determinedly fell on their own sharp machetes
slitting their own throats and ripping open their own bellies
spilling out the shame and disgrace
and bruised honor
that flowed with the quickly clotted heavy blood

because they felt they had failed to successfully protect
their sons and their daughters
and wives and sisters
and aunts and uncles
from the clutches of the slavers
through the smoke of their rifle fire

and in the confusion of African mercenaries on horseback
swooping up screaming girls
and trampling terrified, barely crawling babies
who didn't have even half a chance
under the weight of those mud crusted hoofs?

We always speak of those who were taken away
while failing to acknowledge those who were left behind...

And who gives a thought to those
old ones who had *'the sight'*
and
had *read the bones*
and deciphered the shells of *divination*
and understood the un-doubt-able Truth of Prophesy
that said
the **Cycle of Despair** had arrived
and would continue unabated through generations to come

And who knew that there were those among themselves
who secretly rejoiced in their hearts
with the KNOWING that one day
centuries later
the Blood of those kidnapped Africans
would fly through the clouds
above churning waves and shark infested waters

and bring the
JOY and BLESSINGS
and
ANCIENT KNOWLEDGE
back to those who had been left behind to mourn and get lost in
terrible grief

Indeed it is
WE,
WAREJEAJI.
who are marked with the
Signs of the Ancients

Indeed
it is **WE** who have returned!

ANCESTRAL COURAGE – *is dedicated to the communities in Black America where many of my family members and Diaspora tribe are.*

May the Ancestors protect their children and give those children courage and strength in these terrible times in so many cities in America.

May there be unity among the generations and a sharing of love and caring and effective strategies and agreed upon solutions!

May there be an abundance of life altering epiphanies among those who will grow the cadres of KNOWERS who will change the world in unique and effective ways.

May communities around the world realize the Wisdom of the Ancestors and may we have each other's backs in time of need!

May the Creator, the Ancestors and the Orisha hear my prayer...

Ase! Ase!

Ase O!

Ancestral Courage

The Courage of our Ancestors is embedded
in our DNA
and comes out in many ways

Sometimes
in RAGE
and
rock throwing sprees
causing mothers to shout
'Lawd Have Mercy!'
down on bruised and lacerated knees

Men and Women are forced to duck bullets
and
taser dives
while police play Russian roulette with our youth,
our precious Black Lives!

This world is dying but there ARE those
still thriving
'cause they're somehow living
off the GRID

Building Unity
and
Might
doing MORE than *just* surviving...

They're walking
and building
in Powerful *Egungun* Light!

Egungun is a Yoruba word for *Ancestors*

EGUNGUN TRIBE AND CREW – *is the result of the visions that came to me as my father was making his transition into the Realm of the Ancestors.*

Dad was 94 years 'young' as he would refer to his age. He always reminded me of that when I would say 94 years 'old'!

And indeed, Dad was always young in spirit all his life!

Dad came to be with us here in Tanzania in 2018. We had the blessing of his living here for three years before his transition.

Not a week would go by without him lamenting that his wife, my mother, wasn't here in Tanzania, in Imbaseni Village, to enjoy life with him.

DANG!!!

I miss my dad so very much.

Mzee Sterling Emanuel Hill, Sr.
Jan. 18, 1927 – Feb. 10, 2021

Egungun Tribe and Crew

They were waiting at the Blue River...
Waiting to Welcome Dad back home

Our *Egungun!* Our *Egungun*!
Haaa!! I see them three thousand strong!

They were waiting at that Blue River
with foaming crests of gold and white

I could see them shouting and guiding Dad
with beautiful strong voices
urging him to come into that shimmering light
that surrounded them and enveloped him
and the joy that I witnessed
was palpable to my ears and soothing to my sight

There was Dad's Mother, Mama Ester Honeysucker,
dressed in her finest Pentecostal white robe
Who Dad hadn't seen for more than nine decades
since he was a child of just nine years old!

And there was Grandfather Lee Hill
who survived AND out lived all his three wives
He was dressed to the nines
in his silk shirt and gold spun suspenders AND
his panama straw fedora crown of white

And there were Dad's sisters and brothers,
eight among the three thousand singing
"Those gates are open our son, our brother!
We got your back like none, none other!"

The jangling tambourines were backing those voices
and the drum sound resounded like centuries before
Everybody had smiles of joy and blessings
as they stomped and sang and shouted out to welcome Dad home
through the gates of those widely opened doors!

Dad's eyes flickered and rolled back in his head
As I told him over and over
to not be afraid!

I held his hand and moaned and sang the ancient songs to him
and Ancestor voices resounded as they sang
"Come on Sterling Emanuel! We been waiting for you!
We got your back...
We got your front...
Heck, this is your Clan
And
your Crew!"

I know that time is irrelevant in Spiritual matters
it's true
It seems all this happened at least a thousand years ago
but
the days have added up to have been just 32!

Dad heard *Egungun* sing that the timing was blessed...
yes, the timing was right
and he settled right into that long sacred flight!

But before he closed his eyes and took his last and final breath
a huge swirling wind from *Iya Oya* blew right outside Dad's door
Ushering him in to new adventures on the other side of death
Dad inhaled in relaxed peace for a few moments it seemed
then his last inevitable exhalation
was softly and gently achieved...

Memories of Uncle Bobby

Living in another country, halfway across the world, necessitates
creative ways to stay in touch with family and friends!
I thank God that I have lived to see the advent of internet
communication
and that I learned how to use it!
This message about my Uncle Bobby was read at his
homegoing/funeral several years ago.

Greetings to all my family!
Good memories of our dear Uncle Bobby are many. I must say that
he was the 'coolest' uncle that anybody could ask far...always dressed
so beautifully from head to toe...always with a joke and a laugh for
us...always smiling and playful.

Uncle Bobby was usually the life of the party and I loved being in his
space whether at our many Hill Family reunions when I was growing
up or at some of the family gatherings that he and Aunt Connie
would sometimes host at their home. There was always sure to be
fun and excitement if Uncle Bobby was involved!

I am blessed to recall that despite the terrible disease that overtook
the person who was Uncle Bobby, that the last time I saw him in April
this year, he still knew who I was and there was a flash of the person
that he had been...still joking and laughing and teasing. That is how I
will remember my Uncle Bobby. And I pray that the good memories
that we all share of him will keep your spirits lifted up as he takes his
place among our family in the Realm of the Ancestors.

May Uncle Bobby rest in peace and pleasure among the love spirits
who watch over us.

We will never forget him!

With love and blessings for you all sent from the foothills of Mt Meru outside of Arusha, Tanzania east Africa,

Charlotte Hill O'Neal, Pete O'Neal, Malcolm and Ann O'Neal and the United African Alliance Community Center extended family in Tanzania

My Aunt Velma

Greeley...Alice...Lafayette...Quindaro...
Street names that take me back
blurring memories of more than sixty years ago

Memories of my Aunt Velma...
(forever thirty-something in my head)

And my mind's video clipped Technicolor memory files
upload as snapshots of Aunt Velma...
The epitome of confidence and grace
elegance and style

White gloves and T-strapped satin gown
Back straight
and
chin held queenly high...
REGAL....

My Aunt Velma was flyyyyyy!

And that voice!
That distinctive way she had of speaking
Pronouncing each and every word
Properly and with feeling

Moving her neck and tilting her head an Nth degree
while
fluttering her hands and eyelids just so...
just so...
And I Looooved to hear my Aunt Velma speak!

Memories of Aunt Velma sitting on a white painted porch chair
At the house on Alice Street
Keeping cool in red stripped Bermuda shorts
and cotton blouse
Enjoying a Kansas City breeze way out of the sun

And us
The cousins...
out in the back yard in Grandfather Hill's garden
crashing through patches of green beans
and peas and collards

And us just hollering and laughing
and teasing and running fast
and going *buck wild* all out in the sun!

And my Aunt Velma
standing in the shadowed backyard
watching us
feeling all happy and smiling

And sunlight spotlighting the smoky elegance
trailing from her cigarette
and her crystal jelly jar of ruby tinted lemonade

And She watches...

Some Sunday Ol' Skool Flow...

"...But we can't leave the ones out who inform our DNA....
Our Ancestors, Our Egungun or however you want to say!...

We can't forget the ancient memories that take us back to the
Source... Remember the Nature Spirits called Orisha and shout their
names til we get hoarse!...

We must Remember to honor our Ancestors and say their names
Loud and Clear...
We must never forget to call their names out loud so they can always
hear...

We need to know that Sankofa takes us way, way, way, way back!
We must teach our children with positive examples and fill in the
gaps that they lack!...

We must walk the way of the New World and build the Unity we
Crave...
We must carry ourselves in such a way that will elevate our legacies
from the grave...

Stop ignorance and self doubt and all those things that keep us
pinned to the ground...
We rise up and take others with us as we soar into futures profound
with meaning and blessings and unique creativity,

of this I have no doubt...
Together WE'LL MAKE IT, We always have and this I'll always SHOUT
OUT!!"
BLACK LIVES MATTER!

Portrait of a Good Woman

I paint a portrait of a GOOD WOMAN...Source of an overflowing
fountain of Love...
I PAINT A PORTRAIT OF MAMA...

I fill each corner of the portrait with the coolest of purple hues,
antique gold
and the Lady Pink of her Aquarius Spirit,
for she had a creative gift, an astonishing ability to gently nudge the
plainest of objects into just the 'right' angle to transform a darkened
corner
into gold flaked brilliance

And paint in a smile so real...so genuine in its positive warmth
that any down-turned lips in her orbit reflexively lifted through the
magnetic pull of
her irresistible joy

Search through that palette of paint for just the right color for the
eyes that spoke volumes
through the quickest flicker or sidelong glance.

Expressive looks that let you KNOW when you weren't doing the right
thing!
Caressing glances, tightening silken bands of Love 'round so many
hearts...

And pile on the gold and metallic silver paints to bring out the electric
magic sparking
from hands ever eager to raise the roof with piano sounds of gospel
glory

soothing weary souls with holy exaltations and whispering notes
like angels breath

Oh YES...AN ANGEL WALKED AMONG US!
A life well lived in magnificent rehearsal for the glory to come!

And I paint her transformed at the moment of her passing...

An eager, white feathered dove with splashes of purple and gold
tipped beak
dipping her wings in farewell as she smoothly glides through the
opened curtains,
adjusting her new set of wings to fit as comfortably as the 'piano
fingers'
she once wore among us.

She had no need to look back as she flew.
She had made her peace with no regrets.

And the cutwork gauze curtains flutter as she quickens her flight,
eager for new beginnings!

In Memory of my Mother,
Theresa Calzetta Garrett Hill
January 28, 1928 - January 7, 1997

SANKOFA

Nirudishe mahale mazuri where my Ancestors walked!
Look at my tattoos that I'm honored to carry
They're *Andinkra* symbols representing
lugha that my *Egungun* talked

DNA *yangu,* that thick red blood that flows with life force
all through my veins,
teaches me and guides me
and loves
and protects me
through the violence inside of
the reign
of
despots and dictators
and
racist police
and
those who wish me great harm!

Nimechoka! Ehhhh...
Nimechoka!
Nataka kurudi Africa
the land where my Ancestors were born!

I feel them calling me home
through the Red Blood memories
that flow and run through my veins...
with demands that I sink my toes in
and
deeply submerge my heart in
the richest black soil that my Ancestors still claim.

Nimechoka...Nimechoka...
lakini
I'm coming back home!

Nimechoka lakini
I'm coming back home

We called her Mother

We called her 'Mother' even though she was our grandmother

That's what HER daughter, our Mother, called her and we simply
followed suit

I remember Mother would work two and three jobs
cleaning, waiting tables, cooking, sewing in factories
anything domestic
that might put a little something in her pocket and on her table
and she did it well and lived well

She was a model of an enterprising, determined spirit

I can remember Mother's hands
always looked swollen and reddish and sore
and tender to the touch
from the hard work that she did

Her hands smelled all the time to me
of bleach and soap

BUT

On Sundays
Mother would bring out her
'Sunday-go-to-meeting' clothes
and
she'd be transformed!

The fur coats and veil covered, feathered hats
and
lace accented suits and pearls 'round her neck

helped to give her a touch of luxury
in the harsh world of work that she usually inhabited

I remember how Mother LOVED her plants!
She reveled in her green thumb
and she always had tomatoes and onions and greens
growing in her garden out back

She always had large pots and cans of plants and bright flowers on
her porch at 1121 Richmond

Mmmmm, 1121...
I remember Mother's house so well
The clean smells
the quiet
the shadows and sunlight
and how everything was always exactly in its place

I loved the way her soft, white sheer curtains would blow
and dance in the wind
and
I loved the snapping sound of the window shades when Mother
would raise them in the morning

I loved the quilts on her bed and only found out years later
that she sewed some of them herself!

I loved her joy
when she'd get excited listening to her favorite baseball team
(I guess it must have been the Kansas City A's back then)
shouting at the radio
urging them on
berating them when they weren't doing so well
Mother LOVED her baseball!

I loved when my sister, Sharon, and I would go to Mother's
sometime over the weekend,
way before Sterling, Jr. was born

Sharon loved to bang my head though,
Especially over the right eye,
on the beautifully carved wood trim
on Mother's fancy French provincial couch

Mother would calm my tears
and we'd all head to the grocery store around the corner
in Mother's light green Chevrolet

It was always an adventure riding with Mother because she drove
FAST!
sometimes like she was on a do or die race track!

She'd always allow us to pick all the good tasting junk food
that we wanted!
Then we'd drive back to 1121 and feast on
chocolate chip ice cream and potato chips
vanilla cookies and fried lunch meat sandwiches
with slathers of mayo!

But the *real* feasts at Mother's
were during the holidays
when family members would all gather at her home
for turkey and dressing
sweet potatoes with golden baked marshmallows on top
and the lightest rolls in the world
(other than MY Mama's)
and her specialty...
a whole-cranberry salad stiff but shaky

with gelatin and packed with mandarin oranges
and all kinds of fruit and nuts...mmmmm!!

I loved to help set the table with Mother's heavy silverware
that she would bring out from velvet lined wooden cases
just for the occasion
along with heavy, cut crystal goblets
and gravy bowls and china platters

And Mother would pray...
and THAT Lady could pray Y'all!
Her voice would rise and ebb and flow
with strong emotion
as she'd bless the gathering

And I remember decades later
the prayer that Mother offered softly
in the stunned silence surrounding us
as we stood round the bedside of her daughter,
MY Mother,
who had just taken HER last breath...

And now, Mother has taken hers...
the last breath of a Good Woman
sometimes stern
but always ready to laugh,
a booming
cackling laugh
that now,
I will only hear in far off memories

I will treasure those memories of Mother,
my Grandmother,
Ethel Leona Garrett...
a good, hard working woman...
now gone home to rest in the Realm of Our Ancestors

**Dedicated to Ethel Leona Garrett, my Grandmother,
who made her transition in 2009.
May she rest in peace in the Realm of the Ancestors!**

We Remember!

That sound! That Sound brings that dream on again...
A dream that I can NOT wipe from my mind...mind...mind...
Middle Passage memories still twisting in my DNA!

And it begins...

I watch the sea gull tip his wings slightly to the right as he hovers over
the windswept ocean waves
It looks back briefly at me, beckoning me to follow over the blue grey
expanse of water

I hold on to the slippery tufts of belly feathers
and immediately feel the steely grip of my Ancestors wrap tightly
'round my waist,
lockin' me in...
bucklin' me up...
for a ride back in time

And it begins....

My senses radar in on a faintly heard squawk, (I think it another bird)

Then...
a SCREECH...

a SCREAM...

SCREAMING CRIES
of ten thousand voices calling out to me in languages I cannot
decipher!!!
NISAIDIE!!!! HELPPPPP!!!

NISAIDIEEEEEE!!!!!
tortures my ears and I reach out to cradle the blood covered,
freshly born baby squeezed out in a desperate attempt to preserve a
life...
ANY life...
on that ship that's going down, down...down...
Crashing and drowning 9,999 souls in one swift swoop of disaster!

I hold tightly to that blood-soaked baby hand
its black skin glistening and slippery with the broken womb water of
its Mother's parting life force

I hold tightly to that shivering new born life as we barely escape
together,
that swiftly spinning whirlpool of destruction
...and screams... and cries... and curses... and prayers

For FREEDOM!

For ESCAPE!

For RELEASE!

Strangled out in a thousand languages

And I absorb it all quickly...
QUICKLY!
before the ocean covers them and wraps them tightly in a burial
shroud
of icy, stinging salt water
My tears drip into the ocean as I bear witness to thousands of hopes
denied,
thousands of dreams unrealized, thousands of children unborn!

My hot steaming tears drip swiftly and freely flooding the baby's face
that I cradle in my arms,

cleaning it... warming it up...

It wakes quickly, all its senses alert, and it reaches up to touch my
face,
brushing through the flowing bucket of tears pouring down

It's tiny, strong, dark brown hand comforts MY grief
and turns MY face around...Lifts MY chin
strengthening ME

And the baby smiles up at me

I'm ASTONISHED!

Nearly lose my grip at the shocking revelation
that
I'm looking into the eyes of my Great, Great, GRANDMOTHER!!!!!

She smiles up at me and urges the bird to fly faster
with strongly felt kicks from her tiny baby feet

And we fly higher over the still swirling oceans waves

And we fly faster... and harder and faster... and faster

And
drowned hopes

and
dreams

and creativity

and knowledge

and love

RISE UP
...like hot steam!

Enveloping us...Penetrating...

And we soar higher...
Carrying them with us, securely hammered into the marrow of our
bones!

We circle the waves one last time
and the ocean is quiet now
with a collective sigh of relief

And they sleep,
knowing we will NEVER forget them...

They rest,
at peace,
knowing we will ALWAYS honor them...

They smile with pain free love,

Knowing that...

WE REMEMBER!

Snapshots and Daddy

Early Snapshot

Little Girl Hands securely gripped by Young Father's rough hewn
Working man's palm

Immaculately manicured Fingertips
thick digit wrapped with Wedding Band Gold

Hands holding a silver plated stop watch
clicking off important minutes
Timing our school drill descent down spider webbed
steel fire escapes

Soft white cotton gloves,
pearl button tipped
One on...One off...
Against a background wrist of Africa's riches, darkest hues

And I stand erectly Tall
and Proud
In imitation of the Blue Suited Fireman

Rows and Rows of Shiny Silver Buttons
Visored Hat positioned low in military precision
casting shadowed slant on
West African features of a North End Prince

And me,
excitedly nudging friends with lightly greased and pointy elbows,
Letting ALL know in Stereophonic Stage Whispers,
"THAT'S MY DADDY!"

Later Snapshots

Seven decades of life experiences
vividly etched into fingertip swirls

Hands as familiar with hammer and saw
and
nurturing needs of delicately rooted plants
As they are with thread and needle,
pink flowered china cups
and
red enameled frying pans

Hands always eager to grip life's new experience
Reeling them in…
Like a fish tenderly holding a padded hook
by softly smiling lips
Reeling them In…
Reeling them In…
Concentric Circles Spreading

Future Snapshots

I'll stand in an open doorway
and watch
those strongly veined, sometimes peeling hands,
fling the Red and Black plaid Elder's Blanket
'round shoulders carried wide and open
for new possibilities
He radars in on trilling birdsong…
the blanket keeps him warm as he strolls forward
CONFIDENT
Under diamond drenched sky
in the cool breeze
of an African Night

II.   HOMAGE TO A FEW FREEDOM FIGHTERS

WE CARRY THAT MAROON BLOOD!

THAT BLOOD THAT TURNED THE OCEANS RED!

THE SAME BLOOD THAT HARRIOT TUBMAN SHED!

THE SAME BLOOD THAT MY

GREAT UNCLE ROBERT LEE HILL SHED!

THE SAME BLOOD THAT MY

BLACK PANTHER COMRADES SHED!

THE SAME BLOOD THAT CONTINUES TO NOURISH THE LAND IN

AFRICA...THE AMERICAS...AND WHERE EVER OPPRESSED

PEOPLE ARE ON THE PLANET!

FREEDOM FIGHTERS...RAISE YOUR BANNER HIGH!

FREE ALL POLITICAL PRISONERS!

TUKO PAMOJA!

I Imagine

...And THIS is For Mumia...

You might wanna call him
BROTHER Mumia, Word Warrior for the People
and
Brother behind the exceptions that gave birth to
THE
'Mumia Exception'
Or
You might want to refer to him as COMRADE Mumia,
Voice of the Voiceless

Once a young 15 year old Panther
But NOW...
With crinkle lines etched in the corner of his eyes
from squinting as he reads and writes and identifies
thoughts
that he will expound upon and send out to the planet
LIVE!
from
Death Row

But Now.
..on THIS Earthday
His 56th Birthday
We might add another designation to his name,
MZEE!
Mzee Mumia...
(Mzee in Kiswahili means Elder)
Yes, ELDER!

How can THAT be?
That quickly?

Quick!
Humph....Yeahhhh...35 years in the making, Quick!

But,
MUMIA,
The name standing ALONE...By IT self
Has a good solid ring to it to my ear...

Without fanfare or title
Simply standing alone
Like the man, HIMSELF,
Like we ALL do Ultimately...

Alone
With our convictions
And Loves And Our Memories And joy
That YOU MUST feel,
Mumia,
when realizing that the planet sends out love vibes to you on a daily
basis

I wonder how THAT *shaktipat* of love must feel?

A million thoughts And hearts And minds
And demands
Zeroed in on YOU, Mumia,
All at the same time!
It MUST feel so good!
It must absolutely take your breath away with the joy of that blessing!

I wonder if that is why our comrade brothers who are locked down long
term and went
IN
As young men, inevitably develop into
Zen masters
Of
peace
and
calm
and
Buddha like energy
And CALM And Peace And Wisdom

And
Brothers Like
Herman
and
Albert
and
King
and
Eddie
and
Sekou
and
Chip
and
Mumia

Now stately elders...Urban griots
Jail House Lawyers of the highest degree
Is it because of that bombardment of love

that *Shaktipat-ed* Cloak of love that they wear constantly
that
turns them inevitably into WISE MEN?

And I see Mumia on this day
His birthday
Standing high up on a 10th floor balcony

High enough to keep it private
Yet where he can still hear
the drums and the shouts and the laughter
and even faintly hear the tinkle of elegant champagne glasses
clicked in his honor
and
he's close enough to see billowing clouds of smoke rise up
from
brass urns full of frankincense rocks
and
he's close enough to inhale, just faintly
the sage smudged smell of fatly rolled joints
puffed heartedly
and
raised in salute in his honor
and
I can see him there on that long
roomy wood floored balcony
Walking freely
and
enjoying the sun and walking at a slow pace,
taking his OWN time
to go and stand next to huge potted palms when **he feels** like it
when it gets a little too warm

And
I can see him clinkin' the ice 'round in his fresh squeezed orange juice
(with a twist of sweet lime)
even though
He might probably rather choose a room temperate
Or
even slightly warm from the squeeze juice
since that is what he's gotten used to over the years...

But just this once
ICED...
mmmmmm
The novelty of it enjoyed and realized
ICED!
Mmmmmmm.....

And I imagine him standing on that palm shaded veranda
relaxed and loose limbed
and
smiling his acknowledgment of the faces gathered in celebration and
turned up to him

And we...
All smiling back and shootin' up soft darts of pure conscious love
as he stands in relaxed posture...
elbows resting far apart

FAR APART!

Without restraint...

In the OPEN air

And
With a light breeze lappin' at his face
lifting his locks up just a little bit
and
He looks out at all of us shouting up to him

HAPPY BIRTHDAY MUMIA!

And he throws his head back and bursts out with the biggest
most unselfconscious laugh
and
he reaches out to embrace all of us
with
LOVE
Love...love...love...love....love

I imagine

**Written in honor of Mumia's 56th birthday,
April 2010
Philly**

*Find out more about long term political prisoner Mumia Abu Jamal at
http://www.freemumia.com/*

FREE ALL POLITICAL PRISONERS!

Lil' Bobby... We Remember You!
Bobby Hutton...Lil' Bobby!

That name still conjures up a sense of pride...
a sense of community...
a sense of commitment...
even after all these decades of time

Lil' Bobby...
One of OURS!

No matter what chapter a Panther belonged to,
Lil Bobby was claimed by ALL!

Still fresh images of Lil' Bobby...
stingy brimmed hat set at gravity defying angles
with just the right kind of tilt that let you know that this brother was
Cooool!

He was correct...
He was about some THING!

Community and Commitment was his THING
and
just like that gravitational challenge
he defied any and all who dared to throw an Un-just-ness
in his face!

Challenge...
like the shotgun cradled in the crook of his arm on those capital steps

Challenge...
like those platters of eggs and sausage

(and don't forget the vitamins!)
served to hungry children in chapters throughout America!

He was the definition of Defiance...
of Challenge...
of Commitment
to making a whole lot of wrongs finally RIGHT!

And his example continues to stir and arouse

His Spirit arises
STILL
brawny and strapping
in young voices
(and old)
From Oakland
all the way to Imbaseni!

And we say
"Shikamoo Bobby"
with much honor and respect
even though he remains
YOUNG and VIBRANT and STRONG...
and 17...
in our memories

A stingy brim...
a strong fist...
and a crooked smile...
a shotgun
and a platter of scrambled eggs
sprinkled with a hot pepper taste of commitment

Lil' Bobby

WE REMEMBER YOU BROTHER!

Bobby Hutton, the first official member of the Black Panther Party, was gunned down and killed by police in Oakland, California, even though he had his hands up and was weaponless!
Lil' Bobby was just 17 years old!

Through the Wire

I heard the tambourine tinkle of the shackles before my eyes met their
faces,
one
with the cool calm demeanor of Malcolm
the other,
with the bob and weave energy of Ali

I was astonished by their ram rod stature as they crouched
with backs to that slit in the doorway,
in easy grace and Zen composure
in a dance like, practiced motion,
that served for easier release of the cold steel handcuffs binding them
or
was that steel hot and fiery,
powering and releasing electrified surges of *Shango* energy
to
pumped up cut muscles and solar powered minds
and
to fingers leaving sweat trails of wisdom on dog eared law books,
searching for 'that'
that others might have missed

And
their strength shone through the heavy mesh wire separating us

Wire that achieved the exact opposite of intended purpose
failing to dim the brilliance of their spirits as they stood there,
let loose from their bonds, tall and relaxed and smiling in greeting
that
changed that tiny walled space of confinement into an Airy Room

a

Living Room

a

Sitting Room

a

Front Room

(or whatever you like to call it),

filled with light and ferns and fragrant incense

and herb smoke

and crowded book shelves and internet pings

and soft jazz purring and wet splashes of laughter out by the pool

(with its Panther tiled bottom)

The prison doors seemed open and wide and surely, I felt,

at any moment

wooden trays full of hot tea and fresh brewed coffee

or

maybe mango juice with crushed ice and mint leaves,

would appear, to refresh our palates

and

dampen the light sweat on our fingertips that touched and scraped at

the wire

And meanwhile,

we stumble and bump into each other's words

and

enjoyment of the four-way conversation,

nicking and flecking and cutting right through years

of 'not knowing' each other but 'knowing' still

and

acknowledging and making real

that notion that a Panther meets no stranger down paths of shared

existence,
only
brother-sister-comrades...
and Universe,
and
a unique sameness under it all

And the wire opens like soft paper flower petals
bright with visions of dusty roads and crackling cornfield sounds
and migrating animal feet
and parting clouds off Kilimanjaro
that we (Pete and me), see with our eyes through
their dreams through our eyes,
visions that have been kept jarred up tightly, for years

And
they (Herman and Albert),
screw the lid off slowly...
finally...themselves...

At last
catching the sharp pungent aroma of three decades of bottled up
dreams
and
tamped down tears
and
plumped up hope
and
wild wet laughter,
finally released with a rocket engine
WHOOSHHHHH!!
of

FREEDOM
flying right out that heavy metal wire

And
the wire becomes a curtain woven of hand corded soft fleece
snagging and unraveling slowly...
carefully...
untangling nightmares of confinement
unraveling...
undoing...

and
it moves lightly (that curtain)
and sways and shivers
under the force of their dreams
of
FREEDOM realized...
at last

This poem was written in March 2008, after a first time visit to Comrade Albert Woodfox and Comrade Herman Wallace, political prisoners who had been locked down unjustly for more than 40 years in Angola State Penitentiary in Louisiana, nearly all of those years spent in solitary confinement.

UPDATE: After an outcry for many years from people around the world, Herman Wallace was finally released n 2013. He died three days later from the result of illness and intentional lack of treatment while in prison.

Comrade Albert Woodfox was finally released in 2016 and is now a well known inspirational speaker and author!

Comrade Robert King, another of the Angola Three political prisoners, was released after his conviction was overturned in 2001.
This poem is dedicated to them, their strength and perseverance and their FREEDOM!

Black Panther Women STILL Step Up to The Plate!

I sometimes receive requests from interviewers, high school and university students, who are writing their class papers or college thesis on the history of the Black Panther Party, of which I was a member.

This excerpt is from an answer to a student's question 'Was it dangerous for a woman in the Black Panther Party to assert herself?' circa 2014

It was the official Black Panther policy that we were all equal and all had 'authority' to do whatever work was necessary whether it be in a leadership role or in 'rank and file' positions. The police were not distinguishing between male and female when they were beating Panthers and locking them up just like they don't distinguish between genders to this day in their abuse. They never have in the history of African people in America!

It was expected that both women and men 'step up to the plate' and both lead and assist in every way and in any way that was necessary to ensure positive and effective outcomes.

We have to remember that there were differences in each of the many BPP chapters across the country and in branches around the world. Members came from every strata of life from college students to street hustlers and everything in between and we were all learning and educating ourselves to be true and responsible revolutionaries, everyday submitting to criticism and self criticism in our quest to live up to the ideas and examples of those we studied in our political education classes and those whose examples we witnessed on a regular basis.

In my experience and that of most women in the BPP, it was absolutely NOT dangerous for a woman to assert herself in the party...as a matter of fact it was considered our duty to do so! It would be considered reactionary to see a wrong and not attempt to right that wrong!!

Both women and men had, and still have, the duty to lead in an **atmosphere of mutual respect and love** without using that position as an excuse for abusive behavior.

III.   <u>INTERLUDES UPSIDE MY HEAD</u>

TO MAKE YOU CRY

TO MAKE YOU LAUGH

TO MAKE YOU SHAKE YOUR HEAD IN WONDER

AND

SATISFACTION!

More on Creativity

Let me tell you something 'bout ARTISTS
Wasanii...Wasanii

We artists are a different kind of people
We need to be alone a lot
Alone to hear the solos in our heads

We have to be alone EVEN in a crowd of fifty thousand
to give SPACE to the ART that's being BORN in our heads

And WE walk to the beat of a *different* drummer
and
WE see this whole world differently
Through rose tinted...Sometimes Dented
Concave lens

Yes...WE walk to the beat of a different drummer
and
WE see this whole world differently
That *difference* gives birth to the Creativity within

We walk to the beat of a different drummer
Both eyes closed
knocking all asunder
Concentrating on the notes
swirling round and round in our heads

We let a quick breath go slowly out
sailing past notes flowin' in about
the Pleasure AND the Joy
of CREATIVITY!

A dust devils twirl with an angel's treads
Spilling out FAST
like HOT molten lead...

Mmmmmm.... The Blessings AND the Pleasure

of CREATIVITY!

Oshun Butterflies

Orisha have reignited a Love...
a Passion
a Taste
for a leaf shrouded stroll through the garden at home
where I used to grow soft feather winged ferns and spiky fat succulents
and sweat pocked aloes and lemon grass
and plants that ooze intelligence and stand proud with leafy breasts
exposed
'stiff strutting' their *Ase* Magic!

I see stems fill with heat
powered by solar fed red strikes from *Ogun's* double anvils
and suddenly
a lone stained glass stenciled monarch butterfly flew at me in dive
bomber fashion
seemingly aiming at my head!

I ducked a little, startled by the sudden action
and it veered off course at the last moment
in turn, startled by me!

The butterfly settled down in the shaded crook of the bush spaces
peering and blinking at me in a motionless float like hummingbird
voyeurs
who sometime peep into my bedroom window in the morning

The sun chased me to another corner of the garden...
Oya loves me in that garden and wraps me in whispers of wind
Oya makes me moan with the blessing and I smile for a while...

Then suddenly TWO monarchs emerge!

TWO of them

Heads up and wings thrown back in a powerful fearless stance and
they dance with queenly dignity beside my cheek...

BOTH OF THEM
in double leveled stained-glass beauty!
and they dance for me...for just a moment or two...
then they go nonchalantly on their way!

I rise up a little from my now warm stone perch
and
whisper in wondrous acknowledgement

"OSHUN!"

A State of Emergency!

It's OFFICIAL Y'all! This is Urgent!

The state of the world today...It ain't NO Joke!

Our options have nearly run out n*aona!*

Ni wakati?? Ni kweli!!

The TIME has spoke!!

We who are keepers of the Planet's wealth

Must regain our OWN Balance to heal the Planet's Health

Lazima kumfundisha watoto wetu

Our Children...Our Leaders of Tomorrow

To value their Dreams...To Cherish Themselves

And

To Love and Respect one Another
We MUST learn to walk the way of a NEW WORLD
Like Mama Wangari Maathai...

Planting Peace with our trees

Sprouting seedlings of love

Twendeni...

Pamoja...

As ONE!

A Few Thoughts on Mirrors, Mentoring and Leadership

We artists are mirrors of society and we hold those mirrors up through our art whether it be music, poetry, dance or visual arts. As artists we are able to hold 'conversations' with our communities about sensitive subjects that might otherwise be considered to be taboo or embarrassing or too hurt-filled to talk about in 'regular' conversation.

Art is so empowering! I have seen village youth that I work with here in Tanzania, come to us with terribly shy, no-confidence demeanors who blossom into confident leaders once they have a microphone or paint brush in their hands and get recognition in the community as an artist! Art can open one's eyes and not only make one see things that need to change (that they might not have even considered before) but also give a person a voice to share ideas and methods to make that needed change a reality!

I always tell the youth that they themselves are fit to be leaders! They themselves can meet with like-minded youth (and elders) and form their own organizations if there are none around them that suit their needs. Indeed, they should take the advantage of wisdom from elders and organizations that have been through the fire and have experience but this is a new era and as with each generation, new means of dealing with adversities have to be initiated and developed. It's not really a matter of reinventing the wheel but there ARE differences in the oppression issues now...ie there is social media that can be utilized; there are more pervasive, and invasive, *Big Brother* tactics that have to be considered; we no longer have the community cohesiveness that was available to us who grew up in the 1950s and 60s era, etc.

I always tell youth to consider that they are able to mentor others in whatever their passion might be whether it be math or arts or science, language, etc.

We can all live the Each One Teach One mantra that we still hold dear to our hearts and we can help change the world and bring our communities to prosperous peace.

I BELIEVE...a Sunday Conversation

One day while conversing I said to my brother who seemed a little
disturbed
about missing another Sunday at his church and thought that he might
not be heard
by The Being who we call on in times of great need
The Creator who we trust in and praise and try to appease
I said to my brother...I said,
I Believe You can pray where ever you want to...You can pray where
ever you be
I told him some more then I told him *Usikalize* Please!
I believe that you can pray in your bed if it please you
or in your car...or down on your bended knees
You can pray on the road in a shadow filled forest or pray among ancient
tall trees
You can pray in a field full of bright yellow flowers and cacophonic hums
of honey bees

I Believe You can pray in the dark or in fog filled light
You can pray til you shout! You can pray til you scream!
But the heart of the Creator don't need eyes or ears
To know that you sending up sweet praise, thanks and tears

Eyes wet yet sometimes with overflowed joy
when we think of the blessings that cover us over the years
Indeed
I Believe you can surely pray where ever the heck you may be
It's not the building...the fortress or the edifice y'all, that draws blessings
for eternity
It's the work that goes into spreading the love and the light to all
Mungu's Creatures

with Love, Right and Might!

It's not the bricks or the stones or the wood in the temple
It's not the paint or the carpets or the gold in the tinsel

The buildings are just man-made...not the Creator's requirement
just mortar, *kokoto, mabati* and cement
Just stand under a tree or stay snug in your bed
The Creator will hear you, Ancestors voices, They said!

The Creator will hear you and will surely be pleased
whether you praise while you're at home or in church on your knees!

I Believe!

This Is For Those Mamas Who Wear Kanga

This is for those mamas who wear *kanga* over the armor of their lives
to soften the blows of lives filled with woe
that is brightened by the kanga cloth
that fills the holes of those who left them...of those who never came
to help them carry the babies riding on their backs in wrinkled
damp...faded...kanga slings

She remembers those that never came back to wipe away hot tears of
fear
and shame
that fall in vain from the eyes of those mamas who wring life's dirty
water out of kanga cloth again and again and again

I'm talking 'bout the old ones...those kanga cloths that serve as recycled
nappy wear
Those once new NOW unraveling kanga cloths
whose softness helps soothe cries of babies dear
who valiantly resist brush and comb through tangled matted hair that
was quickly dried by sweet smelling kanga cloth that had been freely
blowing in the wind
fascinating the gaze of the child left alone
while mama is forced to earn a few shillings here and there slinging
short kanga miniskirts
in hot foamy vomit smelling beer
that's been sloshed on the bar floor by men who grin
and rip at the old kanga cloth that she wears

It's that same kanga that she used to wipe the *uji* from the face of her
baby boy just the morning before
It's that same kanga that she'll use to fill up the cracks at the bottom of
her termite bitten door

It's that same kanga she'll use to rock her now full bellied baby to sleep...
that same kanga whose faded colors drain hope from her sometimes
sunken dried out checks

BUT...is THAT the SAME...
that same kanga that I now see fluttering lightly in the afternoon
breeze?
Is that possibly that same kanga that she now clings to that helps lift her
up from bruised and scratched up knees?
Is that the same kanga cloth hanging from her shoulders that her
neighbors now wrap tightly round her,
as they assure her that *they got her back*
as if she was their own son or their own grown up daughter?

Is that the same kanga cloth whose faded colors look suddenly bright
and new
with almost delirious hope...with full blown courage...with unity and
with community love now fully renewed?

Is that the same old worn out kanga cloth that previously was full of
pitiful holes
somehow NOW tightly woven with tears dried and peeled off
like new mottled skin of a life feeling fulfilled and bold!

Is that the same old kanga cloth that she used to wear before that now
wipes up those gurgles of joy that drip from the laughing face of her full
bellied boy!

Is that the same kanga cloth that mama now wraps round her head
as she lifts up her smiling face to the sun
NOW with pride as she strides with new found courage ahead
into new opportunities
no more skinned knees...no more pitiful woe!

74

A NEW WOMAN!
A NEW MAMA!
with her dreams and her hopes wrapped in a bright kanga rainbow!

Help Heal...Don't Condemn!

DRUGS ARE CERTAINLY AN ISSUE IN
YOUR COMMUNITY
AND COMMUNITIES AROUND THE WORLD!

YOU NEVER KNOW WHAT TRAUMATIC EXPERIENCES HAVE OCCURRED
IN
A PERSON'S LIFE THAT DRIVES THEM

TO DRUGS...

ADDICTIONS

AND

HOPELESSNESS!

HELP HEAL...DON'T CONDEMN!

Detox the Prozac Nations Marching through My Mind

Hot Wired For Pleasure...

We humans are all Hot Wired for PLEASURE
Some get it from PRAISE for positive actions

Some from GOOD FOOD...
GOOD SEX...
GOOD CONVERSATION...
Beautiful Sounds...Touches...Tastings...

In other words, we humans LOVE that thing called PLEASURE!!

Like Pavlovian rats
we too
LOVE to Feel those NEUROTRANSMITERS kick in
and spark our half-charged plugs
Over
and over
and over
and over
and over
AND
In Pursuit of that PLEASURE
We will do just about ANYTHING!

IN JECT...
IN JURE...
IN GEST...
Natural...Chemical...or Otherwise...

Children Of The 60's

But I'm not here to preach...
After all...I AM a child of the 60's

I AM here though,
To take you on a Journey...
A Journey that just might help
to
DETOX THE PROZAC NATIONS MARCHING THROUGH MY MIND...

Yes, I AM a Child of the 60's
From a Culture of MAYHEM, WINE and WEED...

Getting high is nothing new to me

But as children of the 60's
Most all WE had to contend with (after partying on the weekend)
Were things like
Throwing up in our parents cars,
Hangovers that disappeared with simple aspirin
and
red patterned hallucinations
(that we didn't know could last for years and years and years!)

Shootin' Up was looked down on and Crack had yet to be invented!

WHO KNEW back in those days
That
DOPAMINE NEUROTRANSMITERS
Were what made us feel good!

Heck...WE thought it was the HERB!

And
We thought the HIGH was in the UNITY
of coming together all across the planet...

Panthers and Brown Berets...
Red Guards and Flower Children...
Protesting Students in Europe
and
Freedom Fighters in Africa...

Then
they dropped
The BOMB that broke open a Pandora's Box
full of DOPE...
and more DOPE...
and more DOPE...
That flooded communities worldwide!

And WHO had even HEARD of the word DETOX?

The Journey Begins...

I try to keep my Rose-Colored Glasses intact and planted firmly
before my eyes
But
They're knocked constantly askance
by the sights and smells and sounds of my Journey...

A lightness of Spirit and Being
Moving through a Sea of Confusion
Waves of City Sound envelope me...
Horns blaring...Sirens screeching...
Acrid smoke belching from diesel bowels of city buses

Buses full of Faces staring straight ahead
Wrapped in the security of their own Day-mares
Faces staring straight ahead...

Lips tightly sealed and
Not wanting to RE LEASE even ONE Softly spoken SALUTATION
That MIGHT lead to an Un-wanted
IN TER AC TION
With a fellow member of this
PRO ZAC NA TION
Whose Citizens spread rapidly 'round our planet
Like Fuzzy, Grey, Mold Spores...

The Journey Continues...

Encounter with a young woman...

...I'm jolted into reality as I nearly fall over a young woman
Slumped by the curb
on a busy downtown street...
Needle sticking straight up out of her baby toe!

Snot drippin' and mixing with drool
And blood and heroin

And she nods...
and nods...
and nods...
Agreeing with the sad state of her existence

Her eyes roll back from the drugs
and
Visions plaguing her from childhood...

Memories of a bright brass door knob
Turning and twisting

Soft foot sounds of her father
as he makes his way furtively
Steadily
to her attic bed

Memories of his hot, heavy breathing
Drowned out by the sea shell sounds
of the drugs moving swiftly through her pitiful, collapsed veins
and
her wasted, broken dreams

The Journey Continues...

Man addicted to crack...

I see a man hunched over his glass pipe in the full light of day!
Not caring WHO bears witness to his steady search for
Self Annihilation...
Not caring that the children playing in the alleyway
Cut and bruise THEIR innocence on his discarded glass vials

And he whips around angrily to face me
Funky smoke streaming out of his anger-stretched nostrils
making me start and step back a pace
from the ferocity of his snarling lips
and
the disaster of his disfigured features...

And he points an accusing finger in my face...

"Where's that DREAM U sing about?" he asks me.

"Where's MY Dream!!

MYYYY DREAMMMM!!!!!

...melted to nothing like this face of mine???
A reminder to me that my WHOLE FAMILY IS GONE!!!

BURNT UP!!!

...EXPLODED!!!

...from a knocked over

CR CR CR CR CR CR CR CR CR CR

CRACK PIPE!!!!!

MY PIPE!!!!

They are ALL GONE
In a FLASH FLOOD of FIRRREEE!!!!

He grabs the pipe and sucks greedily
like a starving infant on a full and heavy Mother Tit

"Just let me INHale" he pleads
"NEVER EX HALE!!
IN HALE....IN HALE...IN HALE...
IN HALE... IN HELLLLLLL!!!!!
I'm In HELLLLLLLLL!!!!

The Journey Continues...

Woman Addicted to Food...

I walk by and see a 375lb woman rushing,
(quick as her body will let her)
Rushing, from a well-known Fast-Food restaurant
trailing a tail of fragrant steam
leaking
from the grease-soaked bag she carriers.

She rushes to her car,
Looking 'round for spying eyes...and prying stares

She slams the car door
HARD
With the finality of a mausoleum's tomb

The woman switches out the lights
happy for the darkness that covers her
as she stuffs
the mile high triple cheeseburger
into the cavern of her shame

Barely chewing...
Swallowing with an urgent need
in
three
sloppy
bites

She ignores the dripping mayo and mustard pooling on her lap

And she BITES away the memories of PAIN...
From the sharp slaps to her face...

PAIN!
From hard kicks to her BACKSIDE...

PAIN!
From the wet strangling hands at her neck...

PAIN...

She eats away the memories of cigarette burns
in the hidden places between her legs...

PAIN!!

And the harsh demonic laughter from her mother
that always went with the torture

She slathers her face with more and more food
Day in and day out
Stuffing herself with the only affection that she will allow herself to feel

Constantly chasing that
Chocolate dopamine surge of Pleasure...

Pleasure...

Pleasure...

Pleasure...

The Journey Continues...

Him too much Ganja!

I could barely see the young brother
Behind the clouds of thick white smoke billowing all around him
like a closed Venetian blind.

He was busy suckin' on a freshly rolled
BOMB of a spliff
as long as **half** my forearm!

Nodding and nodding
his way
OUT
Of the creative patch that he'd gotten himself into

He tries to wave the smoke away
(As if THAT would help)
Trying to part the clouds that fog his brain and
Addle his artistry

A baaadassss verse comes to him suddenly
but in the time he takes to put his pencil to paper,
The thought is GONE...
GONE...
GONE...
Disappeared like a puff of smoke...

And he hits the spliff again...
And again...
And again...
Trying HARD to puff his rhymes **back** into existence

He stares at me blankly with unfocused eyes

as I point to the graffiti message
sprayed artfully on the brick wall behind him

"Moderation in ALL things"
it says

"You can even DROWN from drinking TOO much H2O!!!!"

Detox:

A young woman FINDS herself again!

I was shocked to see her!
Lookin' CLEAN
and
FRESH...

Lookin' HERSELF again!

One day she just WOKE UP!
Got Tired...
FED UP!...

Snatched that needle right out of the calloused core of her condition!

She got tired of being funky
And drained of all pride

She got tired of people *tsk tsk tsking*
as they stepped 'round her
and over her
and 'round her
and over her
stretched out unwashed body!

One day she squinted at that sun ray beam
raking 'cross her brain
And before she knew it
a rusty, scratching note forced its way UP

(Like a lusty belch)

And OUT of her throat!

And
Before she knew it
She was on her knees
Stretching and reaching up
For more of that energy that was flowing
and
slapping her fully awake...

And that NOTE...
Hmmmmmmmm

that NOTE...
hmmmmmmmmmm...hmmmmmm....hmmmmmmm

And she KNEW in an instant
that
she had found HER way OUT of
the hell of her addiction!!!

With that NOTE
She KNEW!

"Music is MY medicine!"

The music makes me fly
Makes me wanna touch the sky
The music makes me feel real HIGH!
It elevates my sprit
It makes me wanna levitate!
Whole heartedly generate
A vibe that doesn't hesitate to pull you through that door marked
NO RETURN!

DETOX!!!

I Loves Me Some Hip Hop Beats!

I Loooooveesss Me some Hip Hop Beats!
I tell you...
I loves me some hip hop beats!!
and
If I could Rap like some of these Youth
Shoot...
You wouldn't NEVER shut ME up!

If I could Rap like some of these Youth

I'd be Rapid fire

Clickety Clackin'

Eyes Glazin'

Sharp cuttin'

Fast shootin'

Eyebrows pumpin'

Spit flyin'

Sweat flowin'

Smoke swirlin'

BAAADDD!!!!

If I could Rap like some of these Youth
The Truth of My tongue would

SIZZLE
like a long wet finger on crimson hot charcoal embers

and
My rap would

LOW BELLOW

like a reverberating Didgeridoo sound
flaming up and felt in the inner parts of us

If I could...
I sure 'nuff would!

But...

MY Verse comes out Full-blown
Old School
Gospel
Jazz
Blues
Kansas City organ...
a Blue Room vibe slow cadence

that suits my thoughts
and
paints MY experiences...

Ooooohhhhhh
But if I COULD...

I'd drop me some
Hot,
Sizzling
BAAADDDDDDASSSSSSS
Hip Hop Beats!

Just Another Love Song!

People always telling me...'Mama C, you're always singing bout Love!!'

*Yes, it's true...but with all the things that are happening in the world
today, I think we need all of the love songs that we can get!
You can never have enough love songs!*

*And when it comes right down to it...is there really anything else left to
talk about?*

And THIS is just
ANOTHER love song...for You
and You...and You...

We got to always strive to do the right things
and let negativity go
Pick rusty locks wound round our hearts
and let them LOVE waters flow

Bust open kegs of Peace!
CELEBRATE
those 60s hippy years!

Daffodils stuffed down throats of guns
anointed with protestors' tears

And this is just
ANOTHER love song...for you
and You...and You...

We gotta plant
Non-genetically modified
Non adulterated
Non whipped
dried
OR fried
SEEDS...
of LOVE

And while you're busy passin' 'round all that Mama Love you got
to everybody else

Don't you DARE forget to turn right around
and
give some of that love right back to yourself!

Look in the mirror,
look STRAIGHT in the mirror
and
FEEL the strong love
that
YOU have for YOU!
and
Feel your strength
mounting and growing
and growing
and growing
right on cue!

And THIS is ANOTHER Love song
just
Another Love song
for You

and You
and You
and
You...

Creativity...Where Does It Come From?

I often ask other artists "where does our creativity come from?"
Is there a thread of creativity that rings the planet and feeds the universe and we are able to somehow latch on to that creative thread and run with it?

Or is it simply a part of our inherent DNA,
a tangible example of the Creator's Touch ...OR?

What the heck IS it and where does IT come from?

The following Story Poem, RED COCKATOO FEATHERS, brought out the erotic surrealistic nature of my creative Spirit!

During the **POETRY AFRICA 2010 Tour** of which I was blessed to be one of the poets/musicians, we were given a challenge to write an erotic poem for an anthology of erotica from Africa, by one of the participating poets who was also a publisher.

I took up the challenge and the story poem took on a life of its own and before long I found my pen (yes, I wrote it in the old-fashioned way!) nearly writing by itself, almost independently of my consciousness. It was as though I was simply holding on and enjoying the ride!

I was elated and a bit relieved when the poem was so well received on stage at the Elizabeth Sneddon Theater at the University of kwa Zulu Natal in Durban, when I debuted it.

Little did I know that there would be about 75 secondary school children there to receive a Poetry Africa award along with their parents and more than a couple hundred poetry lovers in the audience!

I became momentarily shy when I saw the audience then I realized that there was nothing 'wrong' with the poem and that I had to exercise the strength of my convictions!

There was nothing 'dirty' about the poem, I thought, and surely touching on these topics would evoke thoughtful consideration...and bringing up the issue of self-pleasuring in such a normal, natural (albeit surrealistic) way could help young people not feel guilty about something so fundamental to who we are as human beings.

"Heck...this could even save someone from contracting HIV/AIDS or other STD's!" I rationalized!

And so, I did it!
I shared it on that big, lovely stage
and I'm glad that I did!

Enjoy this journey into my world of
RED COCKATOO FEATHERS...

The Red Cockatoo Feathers

She knew that her time was fast approaching
The disease had spread too far and the doctors gave her no hope
They'd sent her home to live out her last months…weeks…days
But she was happy and content and was blessed
that she could control the time and manner of her transition

She had swallowed the full bottle of pills
(the tiny pink ones that would help her to sail on out of her life on a
gentle note)
and her last cup of honey sweet jasmine tea had been drunk

She takes out her brightly painted little treasure chest box
full of her best herbal remedy and chocolate flavored Rizzla papers
and she rolls the last of the giant sized spliffs that had been such a
comfort
and ease for the pains that had racked her body for the last six months

And she lights up…
inhales
and heads for the joy of her garden filled with veggies and flowers and
stones
and herb

She sits on the stone bench slab relishing the coldness of the hard surface
against her uncovered panty-less mound

She had stopped wearing the thick cotton panties she'd favored since
she was a little girl
after attending a women's sexuality retreat
(more than 40 years ago somewhere up in the mountains of upstate New York)
where she'd learned so many new things about her woman's SELF
(Including the fact that her 'down there' needed to be able to breathe

and feel the sunshine and wind on a regular basis)
And that's when she'd also discovered the joy of waxing her polished
hard wood floors
on her hands and knees with the double glass kitchen doors thrown
wide open
(and her thick cotton panties thrown in a corner)
to feel the wild licks of wind on her unfurled, uncovered mound
And now she sat and smoked and felt the pills start to take her and she
knew her time was near
Everything was magnified…
Each memory
Each smell
Each sound

And she isolated that *tap tap tapping* sound of the water fountain she
had found at the flea market
A sound that always took her back to memories of a red-tailed cockatoo
tapping at her window
nearly 70 years before

And she smiled

She pulled out the red cockatoo feathers that she loved to tuck into the
crown of her 'locs
and stroked them
and smelled them
as she had continued to do every day since she was nine years old and
discovered the '*offering*' of feathers on her window sill

She shivered and felt her now thinned and loosely wrinkled skin grow
spotted with goose bumps of pleasure at her childhood memory of the
sound that had caught her attention one morning
during what had become

her daily ritual of
gentle
tentative
clumsy fingered explorations of that part of her SELF she had learned
was named *'down there'*

As a young girl she had gotten pleasure from hiding among the tall
flowers and ferns
and bushes in the garden
while eavesdropping on the conversations of her mother and her lady
friends
as they sat around wrought iron glass covered tables
smoking and drinking homemade elderberry wine
and listening to down home delta blues music

They'd lower their voices but continue to laugh out loud when they'd
spot her crouching among the tall pink zinnias trying to hear and
understand what the secret conversations were about
so all she could barely decipher were half heard words and whispers like
"...down there" ....
"...mmmmmm yeah girl...."
"...What!!!"
"...mmmmm, sho' nuff! I ain't lying!!"
"...mmmmm! .... down there..."
"...Girl, no he didn't!!!"
"...yeah girl...yes...yes, he did...."

It was only later that her cousin visiting from Michigan schooled her and
she finally was clear of where 'down there' actually was

The 'why' of it was unspoken and not really all the way understandable
to her

but somehow, she had learned to feel a little apprehensive and
deliciously guilty
about touching that part of her newly discovered SELF
And she always made sure the door was locked before she laid down to
get to it

Somehow over the years
she had developed a propensity for the 'forbidden'
and she reveled in the 'taboo'

She even loved the way that five lettered word rolled around inside her
mouth
and the hot cinnamon taste of the sound that always started a tingling
vibration
that began in the middle of her tongue
traveling the meridians of her core
to land smack dab in the middle of that part of her SELF she had
continued to call her *'down there'*

She caught her breath when she got up from the now warm stone bench
in the garden
dizzy from the pills that were rapidly doing her bidding
and she knew it was time to go and lay down in her bed with her
memories and her feathers

She didn't want them to discover her body in an untidy heap in the
garden
She wanted to be found with her feathers
in the middle of the bed in her room
In the house she had grown up in...
Been married in...
Birthed her four children in...
Held the wake for her mother in...

Wiped the dribble from her Alzheimer's afflicted father lips in...
Fled the rage of her drugged-out husband in...
And now
The house that she would herself lay down
by choice
and die in

And she smiled wide and licked her lips at the precious little girl memory
of that red tailed cockatoo
that had tapped
seemingly
urgently
at the glass pane of her window

She had watched it from the bed of her daily ritual explorations
as it dipped its wet red beak repeatedly into the tufts of its feathers
Wetting the beak with its black sharply pointed tongue
Dipping its head as it pulled each feather through the beak
Wetted it and pulled...
Wetted and pulled
Wetted and pulled

And then the bird stopped suddenly and looked her square in her face
And it winked and it smiled at her!!!

"IT ACTUALLY SMILED!"
and
that smile and that wink had pulled her into another state of being
a magical place whose recollection became her periodic refuge
throughout her long life

They had stared at each other
(the little girl and the grey and white red-tailed cockatoo)

Eyeball to eyeball

And they exchan*ged*
somehow
the essence of their spirits

She became that red shiny beak
She became that scaly black pointed tongue
She became the malleable armature of those damp
and slickened grey and white feathers

And she dipped her fingers into her own downy feathers nested in her
'down there'
And she wetted and pulled
And pulled and wetted
And wetted and pulled
Echoing the accelerating rhythm of the red-tailed cockatoo

And it bobbed its head quicker...
And faster...
and she could feel its
mounting
swelling
excitement

And it bobbed
and dipped
and wetted
and pulled

And it became her life totem *in that instant*
her 'familiar'
and she held onto its three red tail feathers as they flew to their
destination together

Panting
and preening
and dipping
and pulling

And she let loose her first scream of ecstasy as she fell from the sky
with the three red tail feathers gripped firmly in her trembling fingers

When she opened her eyes and finally caught her astonished breath
the bird was gone
But the three red feathers
(evidence of her trip into another world)
lay in a neat little pile on the white painted window sill

She unlocked and raised the window and stuck her head out into the
morning breeze
and looked this way and that
but the bird was gone

She took up the red feathers and kissed them
and gently licked the still warm gift that was her blessing
And she buried her nose into the faintly reptilian smell left behind

The woman who was that little girl
blinked and smiled with the still precious memory
through the veil of mist that had now started to rapidly surround her
And she knew that her time had arrived

The light at the end of the tunnel that she'd always heard about
was rapidly enveloping her and she lays down squarely in the middle of
her bed

She tucks the blessing of her three red tail feathers gently

into the damp moisture of her now sparse and fully grey
down covered mound

and she sighs in contentment

and in her mind
she locks the door behind her

for the very last time

Dreams of Kili' and Beyond

The ice-capped mountain of my mind drifts
as the currents and eddies of images and sounds
come together to form shapes of words on paper
and
bursts of light in paint

Images that are rolled and kneaded
into constantly changing forms
like the thick layers of clouds
that Kili' LOVES to wrap 'round magnificent shoulders
like the shawl of a woman
of *some* age

Dreams of Kili' and beyond which take me on wondering journeys...

Trips of imagination
that sometime tug me from my bed at night
and MOVE me to get it ALL down
NOW!
Before the image fades and blurs
into an afterglow of incense and MAGIC...

And it IS magic to me...

A thing of ITSELF
with little control from MYSELF...

A crease crushed into the grains of paper
and suddenly
an image is born

I fling the emptiness of newly washed cloth to the floor
and the twists and turns resulting,
form wrinkles and folds that reveal themselves to me
as new images
to paint
and to sculpt
and to sew!

Be Love

LOVE
is many different things to so many different people
but
what It all boils down to is
CARING!

Whether it be about
CARING
for our Families
CARING
about our Communities
CARING
about the Global Environment
and Certainly
CARING
about OURSELVES!

LOVE is CARING!

And when You CARE about something
You DO what You can
to
Uplift and Inspire
Educate
Empower
Enlighten...

The important thing is to
BE LOVE
and It will always surround you
and

flow from you

touching ALL in your vicinity

and Beyond...

BE LOVE is my mantra!

IT feels like the Creator's Touch

When the

Breath of the Wind

And the

Flow of the Heart

Pulls Me into that Creative Space

And

IT feels like the Creator's Kiss

When IT Touches My Third Eye Concealed

Not Revealed

Behind those white *efun* Marks

That I wear

on My Face

BE LOVE...

Efun is a white powder used in many rituals and blessings in African Spiritual practices

Tribal Wisdom...Not Tribalism!

Sung: Many people ask me ...*Je?* What tribe are you?
Aisee...
Your tribe is My tribe
I bleed **RED l**ike you!

An outsider tribally where ever I go
But an Insider
still
with a Spiritual Floooooowww!

Spoken Word: I have broadened out my Tribal base
to live the concept of **ONE** Human Race

Include all our diversity
while embracing Our Ancestral Pride

Historia yangu imefade away
like tears and fears
of the Triangle Trade

Some of my history was wiped out,
But HEY...
My essence **still** remains!

Aisee!

TRIBAL WISDOM
NOT
TRIBALISM
Peace Love and Unity
NOT
KABILA-ism!

My Art is My Joy!

I have made many of my poems into songs...singing, drumming and even utilizing my *nyatiti* or my obokano or my *kamalen ngoni* as accompaniment.

Creating ANYTHING to do with Art is a great JOY for me, Yes.

I believe that we all are born Creative Beings but many people don't realize or recognize that creative fire within and it just kinda fizzles and eventually fades away into the rigors of everyday life!

But me...mmmmm...I plan to be an artist for the rest of my life! I was born an artist and God-willing, I will die an artist.

Creating out of thin air fuels my spirit and pumps up my life with excitement!

Just think...I wake up every morning around 4 or 5am, excited to get started on some kind of act of creation after my prayers and praises to my Ori, my Egungun and my Orisha ...a painting, a poem, a song, a new design...!

DANG!

What a blessed life I lead!

Pete and Charlotte O'Neal...Urban Spirits in their African Homeland!

Excerpt from an interview with the O'Neal's...

Pete and Charlotte Hill O'Neal have been married for 52 years...49 of those years have been lived in the east African country of Tanzania.

Charlotte O'Neal aka Mama C says that "those years have gone by so quickly. It seems like yesterday that we were Black Panthers in Kansas City, working for the betterment of our community there!" Pete O'Neal was the chairman and founder of the Kansas City Chapter of the Black Panther Party.

The Black Panther Party (BPP) was founded in Oakland, California U.S.A. in 1966 as a self-defense organization in response to the rampant police brutality taking place in black communities across America. By 1969 there were chapters and branches of the BPP all across America and thousands of members.

Pete O'Neal founded the Kansas City Chapter of the BPP in 1968. Charlotte Hill O'Neal joined the Kansas City Chapter in 1969. Mama C reminisces that "by 1969, free community social programs like community health clinics; literacy classes and political education classes; clothing distribution and legal aid; drug and alcohol rehabilitation and Free Breakfast for School Children programs, had become the core activity of BPP members. It was exciting to get up early every morning with my comrades to prepare breakfast for hundreds of children in Kansas City who otherwise would have gone hungry! And we were so young ourselves but we were committed to the upliftment of our community."

Mama C recalls with a smile how she fell in love with Pete O'Neal when she was a young girl of 18 years, fresh out of high school. "He was not only stunningly handsome" she says rather shyly, "but he inspired me and so many other young people by his own life transformation and commitment to do all he could to provide a positive example of what it meant to be a revolutionary and activist!"

By 1969 the Black Panther ideology had evolved into a revolutionary internationalist movement that looked at the worldwide struggle as one of class and not race. "Every Party member had to study Mao Tse-tung's Little Red Book, Franz Fanon and many, many more' to advance our knowledge of peoples struggle around the world. It was exciting to know that we had so much in common with people all over the planet. Even today, I consider myself to be a citizen of the Global Community" says Mama C with a thoughtful gaze into the past.

'Because of our internationalist way of thinking, the condemnation of the war in Viet Nam and the wide spread support of our community programs by progressive people of all races, our leadership was targeted by an FBI program called COINTELPRO which sought to discredit and vilify our work. Many leaders were convicted of false charges and some were even assassinated! Some leaders were able to escape false imprisonment with the help of comrades around the world, but some were not able to take advantage of this new age 'underground railroad' and even after more than 40 years are still locked away!"

Pete and Charlotte O'Neal left America in 1970 and after living in Sweden for a few months, they made their way to Algiers, Algeria which was the location of the International Section of the Black Panther Party founded by another exile, Eldridge Cleaver. Their first born child, Malcolm, was born in Medea, a little town outside of the capital city, Algiers. "Algiers was the hub of many revolutionary movements in those days," Mama C recalls " and ours was the equivalent to an embassy." After living and working in Algiers for two years, they were urged to go to Tanzania by the Diaspora community who were already living there. "The Tanzanian socialist government under the leadership of the Father of the Nation, President Julius Nyerere, was very supportive of the liberation movements around the world including the Black Liberation Movement in America, and we were welcomed to Tanzania," says Mama C. The O'Neal's began a completely different life journey in Tanzania, a lifestyle that involved homesteading and living off the land which was completely different from the urban life they had always lived both in Kansas City and in Algeria. "We were city people," says Mama C, "and when I look back on our first efforts at farming, I find it very humorous!" With fond laughter she remembers how they would dig deep holes in the soil and expect the planted seeds to germinate and grow! "Our neighbors who had actually been farmers all their lives, found our efforts to be a bit hilarious but they took us under their wings and taught us a lot. Also with the help of some back to the land magazines titled Mother Earth, we became nearly as expert as our neighbors were!"

The O'Neal's by this time had another child, Ann Wood aka Stormy, who was born in Arusha, Tanzania. Pete O'Neal became expert at innovative landscaping, food preparation, and appropriate technology including building windmills from blades that he carved himself. They were raising thousands of chickens to supply to hotels; raising pigs to make a wide variety of gourmet sausages; supplying their household with milk, cheese, butter and yogurt; eggs; rabbits and wild meat that they hunted themselves and they finally became self sufficient in their food needs.

"We worked so hard in those days, but our strength and determination mirrored lessons of perseverance that we learned as members of the Black Panther Party," Mama C proudly exclaims.

By the time the O'Neal family moved to Imbaseni, a little village in the foothills of Mt Meru in the heart of WaMeru tribal homeland more than four decades ago, they were finally much more expert at homesteading. They would make all kind of food products for the hotels and restaurants like mustard and Kansas City style barbeque sauce; cakes and rolls and even pickles and relish. "Mzee Pete has always been an excellent cook and he could taste something and know just how to recreate it with his own creative innovations!"

Indeed, many elders in the village saw the unique innovated lifestyle that the O'Neal's were living and started sending their youth to apprentice with them learning plumbing and design and even electrical wiring. "We had 12volt electricity that was generated from the windmill that Pete had erected," explains Mama C. "It was a first in our village!"

Eventually, elders in the community gave the O'Neal's a small plot of land nearly 4 km away from their home in a town named Maji ya Chai. Pete and Charlotte O'Neal established their first community center and that is where they began daily classes for some of the students in the area as a supplement for their school activities. "We offered free classes in many subjects with a focus on the arts and history and we even built a stage in the back of the building where teachers brought their students to perform in front of the community", Mama C explains. "I remember one-time Mzee Pete put our little television and VCR on top of our Land Rover in order to hold workshops about HIV/AIDS education. About 200 people were trying to see that little tv screen to gain more knowledge about that deadly virus! It was around that time that we decided to build our first classroom at our homestead in Imbaseni Village and that was the birth of the United African Alliance Community Center (UAACC)!"

UAACC became a registered NGO in 1991. The first classroom built on their 4-acre farm was a computer classroom. Pete O'Neal managed to build five computers by cannibalizing several broken computers. "Pete has always been a genius in innovation" Mama C explains. "And he worked on those computers and finally made them work! We started out with eight students and two volunteers to teach them who were visiting from the United States! At one time we had nearly two hundred students and more than twenty volunteers, but it became overwhelming and we find it easier and more effective to work with a smaller number of students and teachers for sure!"

"We have always tried to remain as self-reliant as we could but we have also always appreciated help in our work," she goes on. "When one of our comrades, Geronimo ji Jijaga, was finally released from prison after having been locked up for 27 years, the U.S. government gave him a lot of money as compensation for his unlawful imprisonment. One of the first things that he did was to come to Tanzania to see our community efforts and to ask what our greatest needs were. At the time, our biggest problem was a reliable water source. Women and girls in our village would walk for miles for just one bucket of water!

Brother Geronimo contributed $10,000. for us to drill a well and until this day, we are still providing water for our community.

The Betty Shabazz International Charter School located in the black community in Chicago found out about our work and they raised another $10,000. in order for us to get a special pump that ensures we are able to continue to supply water to the community! Even though donations like these are far and few between, it is still good to know that there are people in the world who want to help and have the means to do so!"

While we continue to have daily classes for youth in our community that include English; computer learning; art and crafts; music and music production; building construction architecture and more (all taught by volunteers), one of the programs dear to our hearts is the Leaders of Tomorrow Children's Home which Pete O'Neal founded eight 12 years ago. "We saw a need that had to be addressed", Pete O'Neal says, "and with a Chinese American friend of ours who provided the initial financing that enabled us to build the home, we were able to provide for disadvantaged children in our community. Some are orphans and some come from financially destitute family situations but all of these 21 children are smart, talented, respectful and creative! All they needed was an opportunity in life and we are blessed to have been able to open up some doors of opportunity that will surely continue to positively impact their lives! These children who we are raising as family are being groomed for productive and creative lives that will push Africa and the World to be what it is meant to be...a place of peace, love and prosperity! Some might consider this to be a rather lofty idea, but with unity of purpose, it is an idea that can be realized!"

Pete and Charlotte O'Neal are definitely walking in their purpose and living their dreams!

That Furry Assed Spider!

What an amazing experience I just had...
I was walking by the mantel in my room and saw something move
quickly in my peripheral vision.
My first instinct was to think it a little mouse, but it stopped and studied
me and as I looked a little closer, I saw that it was a huge spider!

A kind that I had never seen before.

But that's not so amazing because I see new life forms just about every
day here in Imbaseni Village...
like beautiful iridescent insects that look hand painted, batiked AND tye
dyed
with intricately designed portraits on their backs...
But this ANIMAL of an insect
that I had used what must have been at least a 1/4 of a can of HIT bug
spray on,
was effin' different!

The doggone thing,
in my admittedly very quick glance before I backed up,
looked like it had brownish FUR like a puppy!

DANG!

And then it moved and I momentarily lost strength in my legs.
The eight-legged puppy sprinted rapidly up the wall!
Its odd color and texture and size and definitely the way he moved
made me yelp and spray,
yelp and spray repeatedly.

I called on the Ancestors AND my Orisha to give me
focus and strength and courage

to get myself together

and

do the deed that had to be done

if I didn't want a now, fully crazed brown furred puppy spider

running 'round my room in the night.

I expressed my regrets to the spider for fighting to annihilate him,

but he had *invaded* MY turf

and

even though he might have looked soft and cuddly,

the way he moved on those powerfully built, athletic looking legs

translated to a dangerous threat to me.

My warrior spirit restored,

I followed him with long bursts of spray as he ran down the wall

and finally through my kitchen door.

It was dark in the kitchen and I couldn't see him anymore

but I kept on spraying and now I was coughing TOO

in the fog of toxic HIT fumes!

I had surely released enough of that poisonous gas into the air

to make creatures that hadn't seen the light of day in ten years,

come out into the open in my room,

gasping for breath!

DANG!

Five Priests In Arusha

Five Priests up here in Arusha...
R'chuga...A-Town...Arusha City
or however you like to say.

WAREJEAJI!
Ndio, it is WE
who have returned
spreading word of Elevated Lifestyles
and
walking in Bliss and Ire!

It's a Culture that knows the importance
of gaining High Level Spiritual Knowledge
and heartfelt respect for our Ancestors
and our Kin

It's those powerful Spirits and those elements of Nature
that all of us nurture and carry deep within

It's the lessons learned from the Matriarchs and our Ancient Spiritual
Mothers
that STILL race through the Ancient Braille of our DNA
It's the teachings of the Matriarchs and of our Spiritual Mothers
That snatches us back on to righteous paths
when we falter, fall down and when we go astray

It's a Culture that teaches us to learn and to recognize
that it's not about the gold that drips
not even the silks, the lace or shiny embroidered threads
when you choose the path of your Destiny
wearing crowns of *Iwa Pele* on your Heads!

It's a serious commitment filled with lifetimes of promise
when you embrace your sacred *Ori*
to wear crowns of *Iwa Pele*, good character
and walk in your prophesized Destiny!

Five Priests up here in Arusha
trying to be examples of elevated lifestyles
Wearing crowns of Good Character... *Iwa Pele*
and walking the roadways paved with powerful *Ire*

Love Coalition

And it is the ANCIENT BLOOD
of Our ANCESTORS
EGUNGUN

That flows with
POWER filled NUTRIENTS

And then
DRIES
and
COMPOSTS the SOIL
that
CONCEIVES the SEEDS
that
EXPLODE
with
SPORES
Ringing the PLANET!!!
and
BIRTHING
this
NEW AGE
of
ENLIGHTENMENT!

ASE! ASE!

ASE O!

Don't Let Them Take Our Joy!

Sometimes it just gets to be too much...
too much heartbreak...
too much sorrow...
but we MUST also celebrate the positive
in order for us to keep strengthening each other!
The violence and terror and fascism
are NOT the only thing in our lives!

We ARE also CREATIVES and inventors and artists
And
KNOWERS
of the HIGHEST degree!

THAT must always be acknowledged and embraced.
It is who we are!!
We must not forget that!

We must have examples of light
that people can embrace
and
get courage from
and artists are often at the forefront of that.

We must NEVER stop celebrating the God that is in us!
Don't let the oppressors and fascists take our joy away!
They want to keep us in despair
knowing that defeats
and depletes
our spirit to fight against their evils!

Even in the midst of fighting back

we MUST experience Joy!

It is what charges our collective batteries!

NEVER let them take our joy away!

Even THAT is resistance!

We are the KNOWERS!
WE are the Dreamers
and
We are the Sowers!

INDIGO Children!
The Teachers AND The Preachers!

We are the Chosen!
We are the Artists
and We are the Seekers!
and
We WALK!
We Walk the Way of the NEW WORLD!

We Walk...We Walk
We Walk...We Walk

We Walk...We Walk
the Way of the New World!

IV.   CHINA EXPERIENCES

FROM WATERTOWNS

TO

BAMBOO FORESTS...

FROM ANCIENT TEMPLES

TO

SHOPPING MALLS

AND

WILD HIP HOP CONCERTS...

I LOVED THAT CHINA EXPERIENCE!

In 2015 I was selected to be one of the eleven writers from around the world who would participate in the Shanghai Writers Association sponsored Writers Residency. It was my first time to go to China and I was elated to be the very first African to be selected! I was there for two months! One of the requirements was to write an essay whose subject was CITY LIGHT.
The following is what I submitted.

City Light

I wake up in the morning and sense the soft, warming light rising up over the right shoulder of Mt. Kilimanjaro. It comes through my kitchen window while I boil spring water on the little two burner gas stove for my first cup of tea. There is a certain spot that I like to stand in where I can stretch like a cat and be bathed in sunlight streaming through that window which silently trumpets the commencement of a new day.

I cool the tea with my morning breath and the swirling steam reminds me of the clouds that sometimes wrap round the face of full moonlight that climbs the melting glaciers on Kilimanjaro, the rooftop of Africa, and I smile with enormous satisfaction for the life I'm blessed to live in the foothills of Mt. Meru, in a little village named Imbaseni.

Nearly forty years ago when we were developing our homestead, we had no running water but we DID have a wood bladed windmill that spun up 12 volt electricity for our lighting needs. My husband carved those windmill blades himself.

I loved the soft radiance from the light bulbs that was kind of yellowish and soothingly romantic in its glow and easily hid from sight the tough calluses in my palms that came from the rough wooden hoe and steel handled buckets that I used during my daily chores.

I remember our excitement in anticipation of being connected to TANESCO, the national electricity grid! Deep holes were hand dug in the rocky soil to accommodate the 36 poles and thick wires that would bring the *umeme* to us. We had no jack hammers to crack the ancient solid lava flow, only sharp pick axes and shovels to scoop out the displaced dirt and stones.

We were crammed into our sitting room on that momentous occasion...my husband, our two children and several neighbors. We had disconnected our 12 volts and were eagerly awaiting the 210 volts that surely would be a 'step up' for our lives.

There was a pleasurably festive mood with loud talking and laughter that was abruptly silenced when we heard the sentry outside shout out *"Tayari sasa jamani*! The time has come!"

Huge smiles stretched all our faces as we looked into each other's eyes with great expectation!

We raised our glasses of homemade mango wine bottled three years before for this special occasion, as the switch was thrown. I caught my breath in immediate disappointment! The dreamy soft quality of light was gone!

I could see intricately woven spider webs and cracks in the plastered corners that surely weren't there before!

I could see threads beginning to fray on the colorful hand quilted pillows packed tightly across the 15ft sitting platform in our living room that I hadn't noticed before!

Even the jungle of potted African violets and lacey ferns and deep green philodendrons that were set out in every available space in the room seemed to shrink and curl their leaf tips in the starkly bright light!! I looked quickly from face to face to see if anybody else saw the difference the harsh luminosity made in the room but their smiles of satisfaction still remained.

I noticed oval swirls from my calloused fingertips that smudged the long-stemmed glass of wine and I hid my disenchantment as we toasted this new milestone in our lives and shouted out "Here's to City Light!"

Ancient Gardens, Confucius Temple,
Lotus Flowers and Tea

From the moment we stepped through the gates of the ancient Guyi Garden I had no doubt that it would be something of an 'other worldly' experience for me. It was a cloudy day with intermittent rain and despite reports of a typhoon that had devastated parts of Taiwan and was 'headed our way', our group of writers was excited for this unique experience even at our early morning departure. We were going on a journey to Nanxiang in Jiading District more than 20km from Shanghai. After eating another Chinese style feast at a local restaurant that included dish after dish of artfully displayed, delicious selections, we headed out in the rain to the garden which was originally owned by a magistrate during the Jiajing era (1521-1567). It is one of the five most important classical gardens of Shanghai.

I noticed the packets of foot long incense sticks that are used along with candles to pay homage to the patron deity, and I eagerly lit mine. With bows of respect, I gave thanks to the Creator and my Ancestors for the guidance in my life that has brought me to these unforgettable experiences.

The beautiful bronze statue in honor of the patron was ringed by numerous smaller painted statues depicting scholars, warriors and other esteemed officials of that period. Our guide advised me to find the red silk banner that displayed my birth year and there it was...1951. She said I should honor that particular figure which just so happened to be a warrior! I liked that, as my first poetry book is actually titled **Warrior Woman of Peace**! It seemed pretty fitting!

As we began our slow strolls along the meandering walk ways beside shimmering pools, naturally sculpted stones and little niches of bamboo and flowers, I could sense the spirit of the thousands of people who must have experienced the same peace and tranquility that I was feeling. We came to the perfect spot beside the lotus filled water and I knew this is where I would make nyatiti music to compliment the misty, fog filled atmosphere. As I released my nyatiti lyre's voice in praise of the day I felt as though I was inside a traditional Chinese painting and that my musical notes were the calligraphy accents recording this historic moment in time! Then Joe, my fellow writer from Wales, sat beside me on the stone perch and recited a poem that had flowed spontaneously from his pen while nyatiti accented his words.

The lotus and bamboo have been very symbolic plants in Chinese culture for hundreds of years. The lotus symbolizes purity of heart and mind and represents long life, humility, honor and tranquility.

China, possessing the most bamboo planted areas than any country in the world, is well known as the Kingdom of Bamboo. In ancient times it was used for food, clothing, housing, transportation, music instruments and even weapons. I've eaten bamboo shoots in many varieties since I've been here and I really enjoy it!

To Chinese people, bamboo represents four symbolisms: Bend but don't break; Be open and find wisdom in emptiness; Commit to continuous growth and Be simple and straight forward. I plan to plant more bamboo at UAACC to remind me of these important lessons!

A huge stone carving of Confucius greeted us at our next stop, a sacred shrine to this famous thinker and educator in olden China. The core of Confucianism is humanistic, meaning that "all people are fundamentally good, teachable, improvable, and perfectible through personal and communal endeavor especially self-cultivation and self-creation." Confucian thought says that the practices of compassion, the moral disposition to 'do good' and the ability to see what is right and fair and practice those cardinal moral values is of upmost importance.

This value system closely mirrors the Orisha Lifestyle, an ancient African Spiritual Path that I have embraced.

In fact so many of the earliest Chinese traditions are very similar to the ancient traditions of Africa! Maybe that is why I feel so very much at home here?

We ended the day with a beautiful and refreshing tea ceremony at our fellow writer's home. My journey so far has been as invigorating as that fragrant *chai*!

Stay tuned...

Written as an article for the ARUSHA TIMES and my Arts and Culture column in 2015

Transformed

Shanghai 2015...It was the last day of September
and the beginning of the long national holiday that would last from

October 1 to October 7th

I watched the men across from my flat who worked every day

seemingly without cease or seizure

TRANSFORMED

with that silent clanking bell that

announced the long holiday had begun

I watched them from my 27th floor perch...

TRANSFORMED!

Those hard yellow hats that they were never without,

all bunched together as they,

(some of them)

RAN! And SKIPPED!

And I could feel their excitement even from this height that

made them look like over sized *siafu* ants

I could sense their jubilant voices and shouts above car horns and train
rumbles

and their

'Come on Man!! We gonna miss the bus!!"

as they walked and ran and skipped through the tall archway of the
construction site!

They were transformed from worker ants in hard yellow hats

to
husbands and fathers and boyfriends and a few brothers perhaps

All anxious and beaming and knowing

that the bus they were running to catch would take them home to the

countryside away from

sore hands and aching backs and welders stark lights
and the yellow cranes that matched their

sweat soaked hard hats

I could feel their smiles and thoughts of home
and I knew as they blew their breaths

huffing and puffing like naughty children
making little designs on the bus windows

that they felt released

and they were

TRANSFORMED!

October 1, 2015
Shanghai

Already Missing Shanghai

By the time you read this LETTER FROM CHINA, I will be in the air flying home to Tanzania!

I have had the blessing to visit many cities around the world and some I can take 'em or leave 'em...but there's something about Shanghai that really grabbed me! I've been trying to decipher this rather unusual feeling that has mysteriously come over me... (even though I've of course missed my husband and my UAACC family and friends and I'm ready to come home and dive into several projects waiting for me), but man, I'm going to actually MISS this place!

I will miss the super quick pace of life in Shanghai with fast walking people and constantly honking horns and cranes scraping the sky and food that surprises and music blasting. I will miss seeing elders taking the time to keep fit with daily *tai chi* practice and long walks and bike rides in beautiful parks that push back the noise of traffic. Indeed I will miss scenes of parents proudly pushing big fat babies in strollers and elders playing the omnipresent mahjong. I think I will smile every time I hear music with the unique sound of *erhu* or think of the couples learning ball room dancing in the park. The community of musicians, designers, poets and painters that I've met feel like family and it no longer bothers me that people still stare at me because I know it is mostly just unfettered curiosity. I've learned how to hail night taxis effectively and even copy Chinese characters to show the taxi drivers the address I need to go to.

Most memories will make me smile, but some have made me shed tears like when we were in Nanjing in the colorful square full of shops and restaurants and historical relics, surrounded by huge crowds of Chinese people, and rickshaws, fanciful boats and dragon lights and I stopped at the waterfront to enjoy the sight of two women dancing on the other side of the canal on a little platform in the water, that I hadn't noticed before. They were wearing long traditional robes and slowly waving huge fans that emphasized their graceful movements as they told their story. I don't know if it was the moonlight beaming down its subtle energy on me or the mournfully sad music that accompanied the dancers as they told their tragic tale, but I found myself trying to hide the tears that welled up in my eyes and blurred my vision, And it wasn't because of the age old love story unfolding in the dance but because Mzee Pete, my husband, couldn't be there to share that beautifully tender moment with me.

I had unabashedly cried earlier that day when our writers group visited the Memorial to the Victims of the Nanjing Massacre. There are statues that graphically (and artfully) depict the horrors that occurred and a hall to memorialize those who were killed in the Nanjing Massacre by the Imperial Japanese Army during World War II. The hall is located near a site where thousands of bodies were buried, called a 'pit of ten thousand corpses'. At least 300,000 men, women and children were killed! Corpses littered the streets and were seen afloat in rivers for weeks, and many structures in the city were burned down. Countless shops, stores, and residences were looted and sacked."

Japanese soldiers were also reported to have conducted killing competitions and bayonet practice using live Chinese prisoners. Approximately 20,000 cases of rape occurred within the city during the first month of the occupation!

Being in the dark tomb like memorial and witnessing all the documents, relics and photos of the people who were massacred, made me cry because it reminded me of what my own Ancestors suffered during slavery and the terrible things that continue to happen around the world! I was happy to see the huge statue dedicated to peace once we came out of the darkness in that museum.

I've had experiences here in China that will stay with me forever...from water towns to bamboo forests; from ancient temples and palaces to the most extensive shopping malls I've ever seen; from serene parks and craggy hills that suit meditation to crazy wild hip hop concerts.

I will continue to write about this experience for a long time to come and I will miss the friends I've made here and the streets that I have gotten so used to. I will miss the vibrant heartbeat of this city!

Shanghai has NOT seen the last of Mama C! I WILL be back!

Written for my Arts and Culture column in ARUSHA TIMES in 2015

V.   HOMAGE TO THE MATRIARCHS

INDEED...

IT IS THE MOTHERS

WHO

REIGN...

IN THIS NEW AGE

OF ENLIGHTENMENT!

Reflecting My Aunt Geraldine

My Aunt Geraldine will celebrate her 107th birthday in June, 2021. I wrote this message on Aunt Gerald's 105th birthday...

Greetings Family!

My family sent greetings and love previously, but I want to add a few of own, personal reflections...

Aunt Gerald' was always a mentor to me and she might not have even known that!

From the time when I was still a child, I would love to see her bear witness to her faith through her song and through unknown tongues and spirit dance!

I was always fascinated by that HUGE, sometimes raspy voice, that would come out of such a petite sized person and I always wanted to sing just like my Aunt Geraldine!

I love the way she is so unselfconscious and so joyful when she sings, expressing pure enjoyment of those praise songs that always, inevitably spill out and on to those who have the blessing to be in the vicinity of her booming voice!

I've talked about Aunt Gerald' in my poems and I've created artwork of my recollections of her. And now as I get older and a little bit more grey haired, I'm **finally** starting to sound more like her when I sing!

Yes...when I sing 'full out' and strong and can feel my arms break out in goose bumps and feel the follicles of my hair tighten up making my hair stand on end a little bit, then I **KNOW** that I'm reflecting that' **spirit example'** of my Aunt Geraldine!

Mother Anderson, my dear Aunt Geraldine… may you always be surrounded by Love and Blessings and may Your Creativity always Flow and Flow and Flow!

Much Love and Respect from your niece,

Charlotte Hill O'Neal aka Mama C

Sacred Seeds

I FEEL the seeds carried by our mothers

Oludumare seeds

that grow down deep in my heart...

I hear the heartbeats of Mama,

our Mothers

A sacred beat that is not too far apart

from the vision of a much-needed walk

in the warm earth with a rhythm that **builds** NOT destroys!

We gotta plant Y'all

And
Wake Up those Seeds

that are waiting to become Sacred Food

Patiently waiting

for us all to enjoy

Food from our Mothers!

MAMA!!

The Matriarchs Choose LIFE!

And I see Visions of the Mothers...the Matriarchs

Marching in Exactitude
Pamoja!
Ubuntu Steps!

Lightning Bolts emanating from finger tips
and
Achilles' tendons

Steel Hard Nipples
SHARP
on Matriarchs stretched and sagging breasts
that STILL pump out
the POWER that flows between
REBIRTH and DESTRUCTION

Matriarchs...The Mothers...

The
ONE OF A KIND
who carries
the very POT of LIFE in their Wombs!

Which will it be?
Which do YOU choose?

REBIRTH or DESTRUCTION?

The MATRIARCHS CHOOSE LIFE!

I always had a Special Place in My Heart for My Aunt Geraldine

Ehhhh...

I'm feigning for my strings!

Any and ALL of my strings!

Like the heavy Blues Taste of my Kamalen Ngoni

My Malian desert blood churning forward

Like when I play my Obokano with low down Bass Notes

Vibrating to my very bottom with persistent sound waves of pleasure

Like the magically sensuous tones of my Nyatiti strings

Caught in the web of my own TENOR VOICES

that always come to me Unbidden
and
Sound like my Aunt Geraldine does when the SPIRIT BE ON HER

HOLY!
BLESSED!
WILD!
PRIMAL Vibes!

STILL Deep down in the marrow of our Ancestral-Bones-Vibes

Those who KNOW **IT**

Feel **IT**

from the first two or three notes
Sometimes even before-it-happens-Vibes
DIVINE SPIRITS love to ride folks like my Aunt Gerald'
She one of them CONCECRATED MOTHER'S in WHITE who get down
deep
IN-TO-**IT**

Regurgitating the Wealth of Sanctified Spirits inside

and Spittin'
and Shoutin'
and Stompin'
and Spreadin' **IT** around

ITTTTtttttttt...

That holy sensation of spiritual ecstasy

feeling like a most Powerfully Blessed

Expansively Explosive

ORGASMIC Star Burst

the known Universe has ever seen!

In-To-IT

With
Complete Abandon
Complete Surrender
Complete Belief
and
Dancing accordingly
I always had a special place in my heart for my Aunt Geraldine

Facial Hair Part I

I graduated from tweezers to razor blades
at the tender age of twelve
I started 'taking company' and
arching my eyebrows at about the same time
blood letting marking both events

And I remember graduating to sharp, single edged blades that came in
stacks of six,
all individually wrapped in a little white box with dark blue lettering

The sight of those blades nearly always stimulated my tongue
for some weird reason
making me want to lick the razor's edge teasingly...
just a hair's breadth...
barely touching...
like a wildly erotic fantasy or an outrageous dare not quite acted out...
without bloody consummation

REMEMBERING...

My finger dips into the Vaseline jar and smears the grease carefully
across the whole eyebrow
making the hairs lay down obediently...weighing down all resistance

Like the most gently, considerate foreplay...
to the beat of an unheard vibration...
the attendant finger spreads the oily lubrication
then
lifts and spreads
and
lifts and spreads
getting things ready to receive what is to come

Like an expert Amazonian blow dart hunter who learns to make
constant, instant calculations
of
wind velocity x distance through the forest canopy leaves
my fingers learned to compensate blade angle x the grease that built up
before it
like the bulldozer shovel of a snow plow cleaning city highways

Oh, but believe me...
oft times the calculations didn't save me!

Blood would be drawn time and time again from cuts above both eyes
as I struggled to learn the ways to hold the blade at the correct angle
while trying to decipher the reverse image of my fingers
delicately stretching the skin that held the wiry black hairs of my brows
captive
for the sharp chop soon to come

'WILD'!!!
That's what we learned to call the
un-arched
un-tweezed
un-plucked
un-cut
un-*bleeded* hairs
that sprung up every week as if they'd never been sliced off at the roots

WILD HAIRS!

I'd concentrate hard, peering into the mirror at my reflection
mastering the blade...learning to slice not only using the flat edge
but
also the very tip of the steel's corner that required a little *'english'* on it...

a quick twist...a slight of hand
for those hard to reach places

And there was always that inevitable slip
not every time...
but guaranteed to happen at some point in time...

The pink and white meat slit that opened up during my 'careless'
handling of the blade
during my first attempts of shaping the arch, was fascinating to me

It always took a split second for the
e blood to begin pooling
and
dripping quickly in a race to slide out
and
flow away before the tissue plug halted its escape

Year in and year out...
from the age of twelve!! I did it!
...and my eyes got used to seeing the artfully tamed and arched
version of my God given Wildness!!

CHANGES

When I went to Algeria at the age of 20,
in a burst of my Panther Woman's Rebellious Spirit,
I threw my razor boxes away and tried to toss out the mindset
that had led to this highly traumatic decision...
and
I did NOT like the brows that stared back at me!

Like an anorexic mind deceiving 75 pounds into thinking it a 200 pound
reality,

my relatively sparse, naturally curved eyebrows
screamed at me with a wild woman's
I-don't-give-a-damn-what-anybody-thinks voice and attitude
of Frida Khalo, the ultimate brow warrior...
and it took me years
and years
and years
to listen!

But LISTEN...
I did!

Facial Hair Part II

I don't like the skin on my chinny, chin, chin
when it starts sprouting hair from deep down within

I'd love to use 'hate'
but
that's too strong of a word
Dis-like?
Don't-like?
It's ALL so absurd to think that those follicles sproutin' out of my chin
cause such concerned angst to the skin that I'm in!

I started out with blunt baby scissors
then
flat headed tweezers way back in the day
but
that chin hair just came in faster and faster
'til I bought sharp BIC razors for a more through shave

Talkin' bout 'Traumatized'!!
Ain't no way to romanticize
when your man feels YOUR rough hair on HIS smooth shaved skin!
Makes you want to run and go hide
and then
maybe cry
and
slash hairs with razors again and again!

Why succumb to the pressure that puts down the wearer of moustache
and goatee
if not quite the gender that society dictates
and

mostly just over rates the signals that strongly state
on the one hand..
"HE's virile and handsome and strong"
while the other hand shouts
"She's got HAIR on HER chin!!
Sumthin's GOT to be Wrong!"

Then you get those rare women like Miz Frida Khalo
who gave not a good damn what those others might think
You would never find HER hiding behind locked doors
rinsing blood and sliced chin hairs down the drain of HER sink!

Now, Miz Khalo took oil paints and her little stiff brush
and
lovingly painted each strand like the muff above her pouting red lips
and
between her two brows
but still...and alas,
I've seen no hair on her chin
in the many self portraits painted again and again!

It's so sad when I think with the knowledge that I have
of all that is happening on our planet today
That I STILL give a thought to what grows on my face
and spend money on blades to shave it away!

In the 52 years we've been mated together
in private moments and secrets we've shared
It startles me to think I STILL have a problem
bout letting my man see what I cut down there

No, not THAT *down there*
(those bikini cuts that he's seen many dozens of times)

It's that CHIN hair that I am STILL talking about
that when it grows in, seems like such a high crime!

I've often thought if I were sick or paralyzed
or jailed
for a period of time
with nothing to cut with
or pluck with
or tweeze with
I'd be forced to face fully those chin hairs of mine!

When I look in the mirror these days I am startled to see
more than two dozen gray hairs staring proudly at me!

Gray in my eyebrows
my mustache
and chin
nobody ever told me of this fix I'd be in!

But on the continent of Africa where I'm blessed to live
Gray hairs are venerated signs
of wisdom and pride
so maybe ONE day
I'll put facial hair phobias aside

On BEING a HILL

(from a FEMALE PERSPECTIVE)

Being a Hill...

"Sprung Up" (as the ol' folks say)
from a Strong, Sturdy Seed planted in the Red Fertile Soil
of Alabama countryside

Being a Hill...

Blues and swing going on at gatherings
of
Brothers and Sisters and Kin

Hot Talk
and
Cool Music
Wrapped 'round that ONE thing that flows in all of Us...

A taste of The North End

A Blending of Low-down BLUES notes

And

'SHOUT TO THE ROOFTOP OF MY SOUL

Gospel Moans

Music that flows from Our Lady Voices

Not a Bit of Shyness

No Fear or Hesitation

'cause

When that Soul Note cuts loose

Ain't a Hill Woman among us

Who won't
Strut that Stuff
Shout that Shout
And Sweat in Joy
And Jubilation
in Church...

And

in Love...

Strong Women are Hill Ladies

Strength and Pride
Forbearance and Love...
These are OUR trademarks
The Touch that we bear...
And THAT touch is 'cross the water now...

Felt in the driving beat of a
North End heart

Under an African star lit sky

Being a Hill...Being US!

FAMILY...
STRENGTH
And
LOVE

Mother Earth Mantra

WE Call upon the POWERS of Our *EGUNGUN*!

We Call on the POWERS of the MOTHERS of the EARTH

and

the SKY

and

FIRE

and

WATER

WE Call upon *NANA BURUKU*

YEMOJA

and

PACHAMAMA

WE Call upon the Sweet Waters of *OSHUN*

Blow in the FIRE of CHANGE

IYA YANSA OYA!

We're Fired UP to BUILD

a **JUST** WORLD

through BORDERS!

Let BLESSINGS FLOW!!

And WE need ALL the Power Filled Forces

That WE can

CALL UP

AND

CALL OUT
for guidance
in this
REVOLUTION!

In this
ERA OF TRANSFORMATION!

In this
AGE OF ENLIGHTENMENT that is INDEED

A REVOLUTION

Ringing The PLANET!

Lunar Blood Unites We!

Sister Souls!

We head for the hills...

the mountains...

the swamps...

the forests!

Chasing dreams of MAROON WOMEN buried deep within us!

We wield the sharpest of machetes

cutting away the decay eating the earth

feeding on the very bowels of the planet!

LUNAR BLOOD UNITES WE, Sisters Soul!

And WE carry the Dark POTS of LIFE

within our Wombs!

Let the Healing begin!

Let JOY cloak our Blessings!

Prophesy says The Matriarchs Reign

in this

New Age of Enlightenment!

Bi Kidude...She Rides Her Drum

On the way to Zanzibar
hoping to catch a glimpse of
Bi Kidude!

Bi Kidude...An independent spirit
a little mite of a Mama
Wrinkled with age
yet
Vibrant with wisdom!

Bi Kidude!
There's something 'bout her smile,
Lop sided
And
Loosely holding a flaming cigarette...

There's something 'bout her knowing eyes
that squint with veils of knowledge and laughter...

Hurt and Pain and Strength and Wisdom and
LOVE
Seen
Through the smoke of her flaming cigarette...
And I shook her hand
And I felt a *Shakti strength* that moved me to tears...
A strong *shatki* strength
that moved me to tears in my mind!

Bi Kidude!

She whipped out her *rangi* filled *kanga a*nd tied it
Knotted tightly
to her hips!

Her instrument of Power, Independence and Expression
In place and knotted tightly to her hips!
And
I watched her settle down into the saddle of her Music...
And She Rides...She Rides Her Drum!

That Lady Rides...

She rides her...rides her...

Drum!

VI.   HOMAGE TO MY INNER SELF...MY ORI

I AM MY ORI

AND

MY ORI IS ME

NOTHING HAPPENS WITHOUT THE

CONSENT

OF MY ORI

MY ORI ALWAYS WALKS WITH ME

International African Part I

I'm one of them 'International Africans'

who you might have caught glimpses of on the news

We are the ones who are comfortable speaking in ANY language

In ANY Culture, cause our Spirits got flow, like the blues!

We speak French with a Senegalese accent

We speak Kiswahili with a Midwestern drawl

I'm liable to greet you with a *"Nihao, my friend!"*

Or bid you *Adieu* with a *"Tutaonana Y'all"*

The outside of me reflects that inside DNA

That twists and turns in creatively unique ways

Like...

Head beads from Cape Town

Elekes from New Africa

I sport paper beads from Uganda

Labret pierced in Nairobi, Kenya

I'm comfortable picking up tofu with my chopsticks

or eating *ugali* with my fingers

I dig strong hip hop vibes in ANY language

And I appreciate beauty in all colors and genders

I am compelled to honor my Egungun in all the ways that I've learned

I cut off my 'locs in sacrifice to my *Orisha* marking bridges that I've
burned

Scarification check marks from Mkoono

Chin tattoo from Kansas City

I walked in the streets of Shanghai, China heavily cloaked
in
Black Pride and African Dignity

I dig my long earrings from Jo'burg

And my gown and shawl, a gift from Ghana

I dress all my fingers and some of my toes

With power rocks and brass and copper armor

Wrapped stones from Minneapolis, Chicago, Baltimore and D.C.

Sunshine colored Kanga from Tanzania and ankle bracelets
from
traditional Maasai

The essence and bliss of my inside is reflected on my outside, it's true

I AM a citizen of the Planet

Your Mother Earth is MY Mother too

And I Walk the Way of the New World
Embracing the Good of the Old World Too!

My Nyatiti Speaks To Me

I love the feeling when I get into the groove and let the music speak to me!
When my Ancestors, my Egungun, speak to me through my music, that
Spirit makes my hair stand on end like electrical currents
making my voice not my own
and
my fingers fly through the strings without hesitation...
almost without my ME!

It astonishes me
and makes me smile
and
laugh out loud
And my nyatiti speaks to me!

Nyatiti speaks to me...

Kamba Nane

Those strings make me sing HIGH

in floating soprano tones

then

Nyatiti makes me sing

LOW DOWN

like echoes bouncing off pyramid walls...

Yeah, nyatiti speaks to me...

speaks to me...

SPEAK!

Orisha Songs On My Mind

MY NYATITI WANTS TO SING ORIGINAL SONGS FOR ORISHA

Those words are crashing 'round in my mind like the endless salt crested
wave caps of *Olokun and Yemoja*'s heartland

The sounds float in my head like the smoothly sensual
honey scented rivers that *Oshun* adores

My *obokano* wants to splash and swim in the waters that belong to the
brass lit spirit of *Oshun*

Oshun who is my sister...my mother...my head...my hips...my heart...
my ME!

The notes burn the palm of my hands like lightning strikes from
Shango's doubled headed axe
sparking hot words of love and praise and joy!

My *nyatiti* wants to sing original songs for *Orisha*!

The music goes round and round in my head
and escapes through the cavern of my mouth
with praise songs for *Orunmila*
urging a conversation with the ULTIMATE that surrounds us

THE ULTIMATE point of the universe that we know
and will never know
That leads me to *OLODUMARE* essence inside of me
and you...and he...and she...
and the WE that is our US!

Oya energy spun me around the other day
as I walked among neck high flowers

and felt them wrap me in leaves and stems that
caused nipples to harden and flesh to become goose bumped

Eshu grabbed my hand to lead me up that path of righteousness
and we ran and laughed and giggled
like naughty children
toward the light
shielded by the brilliance of white cotton
that *Obatala* tightened 'round us
making sure that we never lose the way
making certain that our footsteps never stray
and even if we do...
Obatala pulls us back to the path
as we dance to the drumbeat
and my strings sing without any assistance from my fingers
and
Ayan's branches scratch the earth
and
tap roots to the beat of my song!

My *nyatiti* wants to sing those songs
and my *Ori* says
SING 'EM NOW!

Paying Homage In Our Own Way

MUSIC...
An ever-present silver covered thread
embroidered through the tapestry that MAKES UP
The Woman in Me
Memories of Mama taking us to church...
Potbellied stoves
Cold winter mornings
Country churches with upright piano
(slightly out of tune but still sounding good)
Choir members swaying to the beat in their satin tasseled robes

Dignified old Black Women on the Mother Board
Their dignity and grace wrapped 'round those starched white uniforms
Lace handkerchiefs, hand knitted shawls
and
fans waving back and forth...
back and forth
and
they rocked and moaned...
rocked and moaned...
swaying to the beat of fast-moving fans
and
skirt hems forgotten
as we pay homage in our Own Way
Blood of Ancient Ancestors creeping through
frantically opened windows
riding on waves of tambourine sound
and freshly risen rays of sun
Moans and cries of ecstasy freeing hungry spirits...
unleashing Unknown Tongues!

Wife Pleasure

My pleasure at being a wife is immense

The joy of knowing that I can
'be myself'
with my mate of more than five decades...

even when there is
morning breath after a rough night;
dusty, paint sprayed feet after working at my art all day;
and TERRIBLE snoring
(most nights)...

and to know that I am STILL loved and honored,
is a delirious pleasure to me!

To know that it's okay to sit in silence or
laugh hysterically with my man, anytime, any day...
makes me feel more blessed than one can ever know

To know that we both enjoy the same sunset and sunrise
yet
accepting each other's vast differences as individuals
that make up the WHOLE that is our WE,
makes me feel so secure and loved

To know, beyond all doubt, that we remain in love
even when we fuss and disagree

To still be able to look at my man and
feel the heat rising in my luscious thoughts about him,
gives me GREAT pleasure
even after all these years,
and years together!

What a blessing our love is!!

*These words were born out of a conversation about the importance of slowing down
sometimes to nurture the elegance of our being...*

International African Part II

I'm hip hop
but still genteel

I'm ol' skool
but I still keep it *real*

I serve up thick slices of freedom shouts
I'm one of them International Africans!

Ancient cultures run up in my veins
powerful voices

steppin' razors

bust chains
like hot buttered knives...

I'm one of them International Africans...

There's Something 'Bout Getting Older

There's something 'bout getting older

that

FREES YOU UP

to be

The YOU

that YOU are supposed to be

There is something 'bout getting older that makes you satisfied with

the YOU that you see

I feel so blessed to look deep into my mirror

and

love the eyes that stare back at me

calmly knowing

reflecting brightly

those

lovelight energy spirits

tightly wrapped 'round

the I that is ME

What a blessing it is

to be surrounded by family and friends

and

people I love

who also love me

And I dig, oh so much

sending out those love boomerangs

that grow

and gain momentum

bringing

zigzag lightning bolts

of

LOVE

right back at me...

again and again and again and again and again....

❖

Written on the morning of my 61st birthday, March 9, 2012

Wild Woman...Warrior Woman

I am a WILD WOMAN! I am a PANTHER WOMAN...
A WARRIROR WOMAN...
A Warrior WILD for PEACE!

And
I will take you by the collar and come up close to you...
and get all up in yo' face...
and make you drool and get wet 'round the edges
for the taste of It!
(I'm talkin' bout Peace!)

The sweet of It...(Peace)

The addiction-ness of It...(Peace)
and
I am a WILD WOMAN! I am a PANTHER WOMAN!
A WARRIOR WOMAN,
determined to make YOU want a piece of this PEACE
That we must SPREAD on to every slice of humanity...
Of family,
that we can reach with our sharp weapon of peace!

And I'll take you roughly by the wrist and twist you back around
and twist and twist and twist
and
turn your mind to the point of understanding...

MWAFAKA!
(That's a Kiswahili word that means understanding!)

Understanding...OVER standing...

168

Who would ever dream that a word so close in sound to a sound of
hurt...
of RAGE... (an impotent curse)
Could mean such a gentle... Necessary... VITAL thing!

MWAFAKA!

There was a time I was afraid to say the word...
so afraid I might mispronounce the sounds
and
inadvertently spew out that RAGE WORD!!!!
(You know the one I mean, don't 'cha?)

That symbol of much hissing negativity
whose sounds used to be used
in careful
and meaningful
and powerful
and heartfelt descriptions...
(now reduced to mere embellishments of radio sounds)

And I am a WARRIOR WOMAN!

A PANTHER WOMAN!

A WARRIOR WOMAN WILD FOR PREACE!!!

Through Empowerment...

Through Pride...

Through Creativity...

EQUALITY...

Through LOVE! LOVE! LOVE!

Hip Hop Empowers Me

I've been a musician from the time I kept beat to the womb sounds of
my mother

And even at the age of 70 years old,
the rhythms and vibes of hip hop continue to add fuel to my creative
fires!
Where ever I find myself on the planet
I recognize that hip hop is a means to stay in touch with my STILL young
spirit

Hip hop is the train that I ride into wondrous adventures

with young musicians,
busting through inter-generational borders
while building community,

respect

and love!

I look forward to the strength that is hip hop
that will keep my head *bobbin'*
and
my feet *tappin'*
and
my words *flowin'*
well into my 90s...
even 100s!

"...and if I could rap like some of these youth...
shoot...
you wouldn't *nevah* shut me up!"

I Almost Lost My SELF!

It used to amaze me that even though
Pre-dreadlocked,
Dressed in *kanga* from head to toe,
Carrying my babies on my back
Basket on my head
Chewing sugar cane sticks
And
pepper sprinkled *muhogo* roasts...
Just like everybody else...

...before I even opened my mouth to speak
They could somehow tell that I was
Someone
ELSE...
DIFFERENT...
Other THAN...

I couldn't hide it even though I tried
And
I almost
Lost
My SELF!...self...self...self...

In my freshly landed Just-got-off-the-boat enthusiasm
Of living in Africa,
I tried to Blend,
To Melt,
Homogenize,
Disappear,
Erase
The essence of what made me who I WAS and AM...

An African,
Who grew up in and was molded by
The 'hoods of America,
And
I almost
Lost
My SELF!...Self...Self...Self...

I almost lost that distinctive stride that signals
"She ain't from here!"
(ANATOKA MAHALI INGINE, BWANA!)

I almost lost my fierce, laughing,
In yo' face SISTAH tone of voice
And My
Hands-on-hips-finger-wavin'-snake-charmin'-
"You ain't 'BOUT to tell
ME
I Can't"...
(Neck moves!)

I tucked that 'me' tightly under my *kanga* wraps
And
Demure gaze
And
Soft, gentle handshake
And
I almost lost it, in giving it up...
But
I woke up just in time...And place...And attitude

I had to learn to remember that the
"I" that is "ME"

Has a history as rich and as valid as *anyone* born
with the dust of our African Ancestors squished lovingly
between *their* baby toes
I learned to remember that the
Middle Passage memories still twisting in my DNA
(causing frequent bouts of claustrophobic episodes)
are as real as the recollections of those who had never
Been ripped from the reassuring womb of
Family
and history
and language
and food
and religion...religion...religion...

I learned to remember that the French etymology of my name
Was just as valid
And honorable
And blessed
As
Habiba's or Amina's or Aisha's
'cause it was given to me in love,
By those who loved me
And marked me as surely as the eternally swollen scarification cuts
Of a
Dinka Lady

I learned to reject feelings of embarrassment at having been born
An African in America,
Off-land
Off-shore
Thousands of miles
Off-course

From where I *might* have been
Had those captors not had such a pressing need for
Dark rum
And
Cotton gins

I've learned to remember and bring honor to the fact that
I'm STILL
The *fly in the ointment*
The
Lump in the clotted cream
The
Wrinkle in the dried cloth
That
Hard green pea under the stack of mattresses!

And after having lived in Africa for more than 50 years...
I'm still
DIFFERENT...
SET APART...
MNEGRO!!!!

But
It no longer bothers me that folks STILL ask me
(*even after I've explained that I've lived in a village*
In the heart of WaMeru homeland...
In Africa...
For years and years and years...
Probably even before they were born)

It no longer bothers me, I tell you...
when they say in response to my explanation...

"...uh huh...Yes...yes...

I do understand *that*
But,
(*now watch out...here it comes...here it comes!...*)
But...
WHERE
ARE
YOU **FROM?"**

EXCERPTS FROM REFLECTIONS...

I had just finished looking at the edited version of one of the numerous interviews that I did during the UAACC Heal the Community Tour 2014. I liked the way that even the television newscasters in the piece (who are notorious for twisting words and the truth), couldn't help but say that "PETE O'NEAL <u>CHOSE</u> TO LEAVE AMERICA AND NOT GO TO PRISON FOR SOMETHING THAT HE DID NOT DO".

I continue to be inspired by the 'out of the box' thinking that prompted that decision in 1970.

A sister once said to me *"It's amazing that Brother Pete thought to LEAVE NOT ONLY THE CITY, BUT THE COUNTRY, way back when many people did NOT think out of the box about possibilities...".*

I wholeheartedly agree.

It took an uncommon initiative to take advantage of the networks of people strewn and organized around the world whose purpose was to assist those using the international underground networks rippling through many countries...reminiscent of the UNDERGROUND RAILROADS that aided our people escaping from the bonds of slavery centuries ago. It took courage to jump into those unknown waters of freedom and free will!

I continue to applaud my partner of more than five decades for having the insight to escape...NOT 'FLEE' mind you (newscasters love using that word also!) but to leave America with a sense of FREE WILL and to LIVE with a greater sense of freedom.

It's that same 'out of the box' way of thinking that saw us become successful pioneers living off the land, learning different approaches to life through 'appropriate technology' while honing our creativity and inventiveness during the many years when there was so much that we couldn't get ready made here in Tanzania.

My reflections continue to astonish me as I recall how Brother Pete's strength and example moved us forward to make a blessed life in a totally different environment of language and culture and food and nature and people, in general.

It has taken a sustainable sense of courage and ingenuity to not only SURVIVE but to THRIVE over these many years of Brother Pete's exile, building on lessons learned as Black Panthers. It's been a natural, organic progression of our community minded thinking that culminated in the birth of the UNITED AFRICAN ALLIANCE COMMUNITY CENTER and community outreach programs like THE LEADERS OF TOMOMRROW CHILDREN'S HOME.

The years have not always been easy but I feel a sense of successful REVENGE against THE SYSTEM that caused Brother Pete's exile and the imprisonment of so many of our comrades.

What could have turned out to be a living hell of exile and regret turned out to be a blessing not only for us but for the hundreds, I dare say thousands, of people who have been able to absorb some of the energy and love and lessons learned from Brother Pete and the UAACC as a whole. As revolutionaries it is our duty to 'work the system' in ways that could be advantageous.

I feel blessed to have been in Brother Pete's life for more than five decades. I give thanks.My Comrade Brother Pete O'Neal aka Babu, my husband, my life partner, my other half...continues to inspire me!

APPRECIATION

I give thanks to all the influences and influencers in my life...

My parents,
Mrs. Theresa Calzetta Garrett Hill and Mr. Sterling E. Hill, Sr.
and ALL My Ancestors.

My husband of 52 years, Mzee Pete O'Neal.

Our children, Malcolm X. O'Neal and AnnWood 'Stormy' O'Neal.

Our extended UAACC family including the Leaders of Tomorrow Children
and all of the Volunteers who have shared their extensive knowledge
here at UAACC over the years.

My Spiritual Teachers and my Comrades around the planet.

I give thanks to the reviewers and the editors of this work.

I give thanks to African Perspectives Publishers for undertaking this
project with professionalism and vigor.

I give thanks to the Creator,
my Egungun and the Spiritual Forces
who Guide and Protect me!

Ase! Ase!

Ase O!

GLOSSARY

Kanga: brightly colored cloth usually with proverbs and borders widely used in Tanzania

Uji: porridge widely used in Tanzania

Kili': nickname for Mt. Kilimanjaro, the tallest mountain in Africa located in Tanzania

je: Kiswahili word attached to the end of a word to express a question e.g. umeamkaje (how did you wake up)

aisee: Kiswahili...used to express surprise or   strong emotion

yangu imefade away: Kiswahili...mine has faded away

kabila-ism: Kiswahili...kabila means tribe

nyatiti: eight string lyre originates in the Luo tribe of Kenya and widely used in east Africa

kamalen ngoni: traditional harp originates in Mali among the Donso hunter society

Ori: Yoruba...inner self/consciousness

R'chuga: slang word for Arusha, a city in northern Tanzania

ndio: Kiswahilil....Yes

Iwa Pele: Yoruba...good and gentle character

Ire: Yoruba...good fortune

umeme: Kiswahili...electricity

tayari sasa jamani: Kiswahili phrase meaning 'it's ready now family!'

siafu: Kiswahili...army ants

Olodumare: Yoruba...Supreme Being

Ubuntu: Zulu phrase meaning 'I AM because You ARE'

obokano: eight string lyre originating in western Kenya

Nana Buruku: Grandmother of all Orisha. Embodies spirit of earth and moon

Yemoja/Yemonja: Yoruba...Orisha of the waters and mother of all Orisha

Pachamama: Earth Mother among the indigenous people in the Andes

Iya Yansa: Yoruba... Praise names for Orisha Oya

rangi: Kiswahili...color

Bi Kidude: famous singer/drummer from Zanzibar referred to as the 'queen of Taarab and traditional Unyago music'

nihao: default greeting (hello) in Chinese

tutaonana: Kiswahili...see you another time/later

elekes: Yoruba...consecrated beads serving as banners of prominently known Orisha

ugali: Kiswahili...heavy cornmeal mixture widely used in east and southern Africa

kamba nane: Kiswahili...eight strings/used in reference to eight string *lyres nyatiti* and obokano

Olokun: Yoruba...Orisha of the depths of the ocean. Keeper of powerful secrets

Shango: Yoruba...Orisha of thunder and lightning and great power

Orunmila: Yoruba...Orisha of knowledge and wisdom

Esu/Eshu: Yoruba...Orisha spirit at the crossroads

Obatala: Yoruba...Orisha who is the creator of human bodies/owner of all heads

Ayan: Yoruba...Orisha of musical instruments

mwafaka: Kiswahili...understanding

muhogo: Kiswahili....cassava

anatoka mahali ingine, bwana: Kiswahili...she/he is from somewhere else

Mnegro: Kiswahili…a name denoting the tribe of Africans born in the west

WaMeru: a tribe in northern Tanzania especially Arusha region

ni kweli: Kiswahili…it's true/certain

yebo: Zulu…yes

ukue mfano safi: Kiswahili…be a good example

BIO OF THE AUTHOR

CHARLOTTE HILL O'NEAL aka Mama C aka Iya Osotunde Fasuyi is an internationally known visual artist, musician, performance artist, ATR priestess, film maker, poet/writer of more than three decades experience.

She was born in Kansas City, KS in 1951 and has lived in Tanzania with her husband Pete O'Neal, founder and former Chairman of the Kansas City Chapter of the Black Panther Party and co-founder of the UNITED AFRICAN ALLIANCE COMMUNITY CENTER UAACC and the Leaders of Tomorrow Children's Home, since 1972.

In addition to her decades of community activism, Mama C is a mother of two children, Malcolm O'Neal and AnnWood 'Stormy' O'Neal and co founder and Director of UAACC located outside of Arusha, Tanzania. Her poetry and performing talents have been showcased on stage, television and radio in many cities in Africa and America during the annual **UAACC HEAL THE COMMUNITY** Tour.

Mama C went to Venezuela twice as a delegate to the 1st and 2nd **EcoSocialist International** gatherings hosted by celebrated 'maroon' communities in Veroes and the state of Yaracuy.

She was selected for the **Poetry Africa** tour in 2010 that took her to Cape Town; Zimbabwe; Malawi and Durban.

Mama C is the first African woman to be chosen for a two months Writers Residency in the Shanghai Writers Association Program in 2015 and she was a featured poet at the Hangzhou China Poetry Festival also in 2015.

She launched her first book of poetry, **Warrior Woman of Peace**, in 2008 and her 2nd poetry book, **Life Slices**, in 2016.

She is presently working on her memoirs and completing her 2nd film titled **Nyatiti Medicine** about a victim of obstetric fistula.

Mama C's love of all things 'art' is documented in **Mama C: Urban Warrior in the African Bush** by Dr. Joanne Hershfield and she is also featured in the classic documentary about Pete O'Neal, **A Panther in Africa** by Aaron Matthews in addition to being featured in **Legacy: Spirit of the Black Panthers** by Taishi Thomas and **Ni Wakati** a documentary about east African hip hop pioneers by Michael Wanguhu.

Mama C plays *nyatiti* and *obokano*, traditional African eight string lyres from Kenya and *kamalen ngoni*, a 12 string traditional harp originating in Mali. She has four albums of original music and poetry produced at Peace Power Productions and Mandugu Digital.

Printed in the United States
by Baker & Taylor Publisher Services